TIME TEAM'S
TIMECHESTER

cirencester
college
a beacon college

TIME TEAM'S TIMECHESTER

A COMPANION TO ARCHAEOLOGY

CARENZA LEWIS

PHIL HARDING & MICK ASTON

EDITED AND DEVISED BY TIM TAYLOR

ORIGINAL ILLUSTRATIONS BY VICTOR AMBRUS

First published in 2000 by Channel 4 Books. This edition published 2002 by Channel 4 Books, an imprint of
Pan Macmillan Ltd, 20 New Wharf Road, London N1 9RR, Basingstoke and Oxford.

Associated companies throughout the world.

www.panmacmillan.com

ISBN 0 7522 6517 2

9 8 7 6 5 4 3 2 1

A CIP catalogue record for this book is available from the British Library.

Design by DW Design
Colour reproduction by Speedscan Ltd
Printed in Great Britain by Butler & Tanner, Frome, Somerset

This book accompanies *Time Team* made by Videotext Communications Ltd in association with Picture House Television
Company for Channel 4.
Executive producer: Philip Clarke
Series Producer: Tim Taylor

contents

introduction

Welcome to Timechester. I hope your exploration of this unique town will introduce you to some of the key ideas and techniques that make an appearance on *Time Team*. Carenza Lewis, Mick Aston, Phil Harding and myself will take you through the history of the town, with the help of Victor Ambrus's illustrations, and provide a guide to the main elements of archaeological exploration, which might be applied to many such sites in Britain.

If Timechester is to an extent an idealized location, I'd like to think that it's not unrealistic. The sort of changes that Victor's drawings record and Carenza's text describes are typical of many British towns. The way they have hidden and revealed evidence from the past is also not untypical. I hope this book will give you a general sense of how these changes appear to archaeologists as they excavate through the layers of the past. Certain periods leave distinct kinds of evidence. This is a story that will be told by physical structure and artefacts, and the archaeologists will be clear about how the changes and transitions of Timechester can be seen in the excavations themselves – so you're not in for a lot of boring theory and speculation.

Many *Time Team* sites begin with a search for evidence from just a single period, and then uncover material from later or earlier times. As Mick has said before, sometimes a plunge into the historical cake ends up being more like a trip into a trifle! It is often a great strain on the hard-pressed researchers that a story that begins by being Roman on Day One suddenly ends up as Neolithic on Day Two, with the result that they have to supply the necessary background information at short notice. While looking at the hundreds of sites we get offered each year for *Time Team*, I have often wistfully hoped for some idealized location where all the physical evidence for the majority of prehistoric and historic transitions can be found on one site.

We have got nearer to such a site in the annual hunt for a location for the live *Time Team*, which usually takes place in August. Finding one that works for a

victor ambrus whose
drawings bring
timechester to life

live programme is difficult. Live television chews up archaeology! The speed of the event seems to swallow up great finds, fascinating trenches and amazing discoveries in a blur of live broadcasts created under maximum pressure. A suitable site must have lots of good archaeology, preferably from three topographically different locations. Therefore we have had to find sites where the layers of history and prehistory are richly represented. The ones we visited in 1999 and 2000 – York and Canterbury – are the locations that probably come closest to a town like Timechester, and Mick also considers Gloucester and Leicester to have similar qualities. These are cities that bear the mark of the great transitions and evolutions that have made Britain the place it is, and it was the search for such sites that created in my mind the existence of a place like Timechester that could bring to life these changes over time.

Archaeologists, when asked, occasionally use the word 'palimpsest' for this kind of site – it doesn't exactly trip off the tongue, but it conveys the idea that some landscapes carry the mark of a wide range of historical and prehistorical events. In that sense Timechester is just such a place but, as a palimpsest, it would be a difficult archaeological nut to crack. If you were asked to conduct an archaeological evaluation of the city, where would you start? It's a sad but true fact that you would probably hope for a large supermarket extension, or a long stretch of bypass to be under construction! In some of our more tightly packed towns there is not much space to access the past, and archaeologists are dependent on a rather uneasy relationship with developers. In Britain the lack of money for research excavation means that they are a major source of funds. All archaeologists regularly dream of emigrating to Denmark, where research into the past does not have to be dependent on the next supermarket. Here, however, we often have to work alongside the builders and pipeline-layers in large towns.

I recall a recent advertisement I saw recently on television that depicted events that were unlikely to happen because they were simply too sensible to occur in real life. It featured a road being dug up for a pipeline. Cable-layers, water-board workers and electrical engineers all decided to take advantage of the excavation and the advertisement ended with the arrival of an undertaker. I always thought a small team of furtive archaeologists should have got in there somehow. I also remember Mick asking a whole series of rather precious clerics when their church was going get a decent set of central-heating pipes laid, for reasons that were less to do with the warmth of the parishioners than with the potential access to the underfloor archaeology.

Getting into Timechester is probably going to be difficult. So where should we start? When I put the same question to Mick he immediately talked about map research. A good map of the town, from about 1800, would be invaluable because it might record a street plan that originated in the medieval period or earlier. Our Saxon and medieval ancestors laid out patterns of streets and homes that can still be seen today. Hidden amongst supermarkets and shopping centres are little streets with odd names like Watergate and Cheapside, which still make their way across the town as they did when our forebears crossed it 1,000 years ago. So Mick would make a start with the maps.

Every year *Time Team*'s researchers filter through hundreds of sites and make suggestions as to which we should dig. The final decision is down to me and, if I were considering Timechester, the other evidence I would want to see would be aerial photographs and the Sites and Monuments Record: the former for any trace of those ancient street patterns and crop marks in the surrounding fields, and the latter because it is a marvellous record of everything we know archaeologically about discoveries in a specific area. I'd also want to check that the county archaeologist was enthusiastic and that the town wasn't covered in scheduled sites. You will find a guide to all the key elements we would look at in this book, but perhaps more important will be the references to excavation. Phil will describe the difficulties of digging in each historical period and use his lifetime of experience to give you an idea of just how he gets the evidence out of an excavation. Each period has its peculiarities and requires a slightly different combination of techniques.

If *Time Team* has shown one thing in its seventy or so programmes, it is the importance of digging a hole into the archaeology. There will never be a form of geophysics that can do what a skilled excavator can do, and the geophysics team will be the first to tell you that their results need to be tested by excavation. Time and time again, it has been this that has provided the only clue to the real story of the site and replaced yards of hot air with a decent bit of evidence. So our search into Timechester will include a lot of references to the physical evidence that can only come through excavation – 'excavation not speculation' would make a good *Time Team* motto.

In discussing Timechester with Mick, we talked about the key pieces of physical evidence. He particularly liked the idea of finding a Roman object with a Christian symbol on it, but as he and everyone involved with *Time Team* would confirm, objects can be useless unless they are found by a trained excavator from a stratified context – or, to put it simply, you've got to know which layer they came from! So the hunt for Timechester's past would rely on good research, good geophysics and – most importantly – good excavation. To avoid being told off by Phil, I should also add that excellent recording of the evidence would be a vital element of the work.

In the course of talking to the members of *Time Team* about this book, I asked each of them to name their favourite period, and when in Timechester's past they would like to have lived. Their answers were often surprising. If you look closely, you may find evidence of these in the drawings. You will be looking for a small hairy archaeologist, a flaxen-haired surveyor, a wickedly handsome Hungarian artist of a certain age, a distinctively dressed excavator, a quizzical presenter and a harassed series producer waving his arms about. See if you can spot us!

I wish you luck and enjoyment as you join us in an investigation into this rare and wonderful location – I wish they were all like this!

Tim Taylor

CHAPTER I
palaeolithic

carenza's story of
Timechester in 450,000 BC

Humans first appeared at Timechester nearly half a million years ago. If you could travel a year for each step you took you would have to walk 500 kilometres (310 miles) – from central London to the very tip of Cornwall – to get back to that time. Since then there have been perhaps as many as twenty ice ages, each lasting thousands of years, when Britain was covered with huge glaciers on which nothing could grow and no one could live. These sheets of ice scraped across the landscape carrying huge stacks of rock like twigs in a stream, filling in old river beds and scouring out new valleys. They left mounds of detritus the size of small hills, and each time the ice advanced and retreated the landscape was utterly changed. But in the millennia between each ice age the glaciers retreated northwards and the land unfroze. Human populations also moved north following huge herds of animals and gradually colonized the newly freed land.

The first humans to appear at Timechester were so different to modern men and women that they could not have interbred with them. They were a form of *Homo erectus* ('human who walked upright') who evolved in Africa two million years ago.

Nearly half a million years ago the first human beings ever to set foot in the area that was to become Timechester were there because of a mammoth. They had followed it for perhaps a couple of hours after wounding it with a hail of wooden spears in a carefully planned attack that had itself been the result of a long day of stalking and waiting. The mammoth had been chosen with care and was a fine beast in the prime of life, but once struck it stumbled for the last time to the edge of the river where the humans had first seen it and was soon on the ground. The hunters were quick and efficient. They killed the mammoth and then set about skinning it. They had collected stones while they were following their prey but the precaution had been unnecessary – the edge of the river was a mass of flint cobbles, just right for the job. The flints had been rolled smooth by the water, but the humans could imagine the sharp tools within them.

Within a couple of minutes calloused hands skilfully wielding stone hammers had chipped away the smooth outer surface of one of the cobbles, revealing the sharp, shiny surface below. Then a softer hammer made from elephant bone – one of their most prized possessions – was used to perfect the oval shape of the ideal butchery tool. Five more such handaxes were made in rapid succession, each deliberately designed to be slightly different to the others. Only one caused any problem when it broke suddenly into three pieces as stone cleaved stone. The fragments were thrown to one side and no further thought was given to them as a replacement flint cobble was grabbed from the thousands that lay around.

flakes of flint, dating back
to the palaeolithic period,
being uncovered at
Elveden in Suffolk

Still warm, the mammoth was soon skinned. The hide was supple and strong and once cleaned and dried would give many months' shelter from rain and cold. Now the carcass could be butchered, divided up into portions that could be eaten at once or carried away. Expertly, the brand-new stone tools were drawn through the meat. One hand deftly pulled and pushed the flesh but the other never touched it: it was kept quite dry so that its grip on the handaxe would stay firm. The dozen people working on the kill were soon joined by others. Some were children, some were very old and there were three with injuries that had made them unable to join in the hunt. They were handed meat as they arrived and ate it at once, fresh and warm from the kill. As they ate the children watched the workers keenly, absorbing the skills they would soon need to use themselves. They were not the only ones who were hungry – hyenas circled, but at a distance. Bitter experience had taught them not to attempt to take the hunters' quarry. Although the humans did not have sharp teeth or claws, the hyenas were more frightened of them than they were of lions or wolves, whose kills they could steal through weight of numbers and persistent harrying. But the human hunters, who walked upright on two legs, were much more dangerous – they could kill from afar. With their closely set eyes under heavy brow ridges and sloping foreheads, set above broad, flat noses and heavy, chinless jaws, they could see keenly and their aim was seemingly unerring when they threw axes and spears, sticks and stones. Their large brains enabled them to work as a team and to communicate instructions and warnings in a guttural language. Even children under five who were too young to fend for themselves could look out for scavengers and throw stones with dangerous accuracy. For the hyenas, there were easier kills to be stolen elsewhere.

Within three hours the mammoth carcass was bare. The only task that remained was to smash open its bones to get at the rich, delicious marrow. The ends of one or two long ones were kept to use as hammers when the one made from elephant bone wore out. By nightfall the task was complete; half a ton of mammoth meat had been stripped and jointed, packed up or eaten. The humans moved away, leaving the scant remains of the carcass to the hyenas.

A hundred metres upriver they made a rough shelter from an old hide stretched across a low-hanging branch near the entrance to a small cave. The hard-won meat was hung from the higher branches of a neighbouring tree. Two people kept watch all night.

In the morning the humans began to tear the meat up into thin strips which, once dried, would keep for a long time. New wooden spears were fashioned to replace those lost in the hunt and frogs and fungi, plants, roots and berries were collected – whatever could be found in the place the mammoth had brought them to. When this food supply ran out and the mammoth meat had been eaten the humans would move on, following the large animals that were their prey. And when the weather deteriorated at the beginning of the next ice age animals and humans alike would migrate south, leaving Timechester to thousands more years of icy peace before the next interglacial once again brought back plants, animals and perhaps even humans.

underground archeology

Caves can be very cold, damp and dirty. Many are dried-up river channels and can just as easily fill up again in times of heavy rain. They can also act like drains and are liable to flood. The logistics of excavating a cave site are therefore difficult because conditions are dark, potentially dangerous and often rather cramped. It is important to make sure all aspects of health and safety have been checked before starting to excavate.

Unlike open sites where trenches can be laid out to suit the excavator, ones in caves are often constrained by the size and shape of the cave itself. The same factors may well have affected how it was used in the past and as a result the most interesting area to excavate is often just within, or immediately outside, the entrance. This was the best place to live as it provided its occupants with light and air as well as shelter.

Time Team descending into the depths of Cooper's Hole

However, the location of the mouth of the cave may have changed since the time of occupation. The rock face may have been eroded and the modern opening may be sited further back than the earlier one. An indication of this is large lumps of rock lying in the entrance. These may have fallen from the roof of the cave and will have to be removed or, if they are too big, worked around.

It is important to understand how the cave was formed and how it filled up, and a geologist or sedimentologist is therefore an essential member of the excavating team. Filling up often occurred during glacial periods when frost action loosened rocks from the roof of the cave so that they fell and caused infilling. Similarly a lot of sediment was brought into caves when the ice sheets melted and flood waters swept across the landscape.

Many famous collections in museums come from cave excavations. Hyenas, lions and a wide range of other carnivores would have taken their prey back to their cave dens – their natural homes. The carcasses would be eaten there and some bones would become buried in the sediments on the floor. Fortunately, the chemical environment of limestone caves is very well suited to the long-term preservation of bone, and material found there can be exceptionally well preserved. Although humans also made use of caves, and sometimes left obvious traces of their presence in the form of stone tools or carved bones, such evidence is rare. Other, less obvious, indications of human activity often have to be proved by close examination of finds for traces of deliberate butchery like the cut marks *Time Team* found on a bone from Cooper's Hole in the Cheddar Gorge, Somerset.

Palaeolithic Tools

Acheulean handaxes, called after Saint-Acheul in the Somme Valley of northern France where they were first found, were the most common Lower Palaeolithc

tools. The earliest were made in Africa some 1.5 million years ago, a million years before they were introduced to Britain in about 500,000 BC. They were primarily used for butchery, but probably also served a multitude of other functions.

Handaxes are usually pear-shaped with pointed tips, although some are oval and others look like hearts, and were made using a stone hammer to flake both sides of a lump of flint. Fine thinning and finishing was achieved with hammers made from deer antler, elephant bone or softer stone, which provided a far greater degree of control than stone ones and allowed delicate flakes to be removed.

Making a handaxe is a complex activity which requires a developed memory and the ability to retain a mental template of the finished tool, as well as the capacity to coordinate the senses in order to feel, see and hear the flaking. So, although these stone axes are the most common artefacts that teach us about our earliest ancestors, people who were capable of making sophisticated tools like handaxes would also have been able to produce wooden spears, baskets, nets and leather goods. However, these have not survived in the ground.

Despite having the developed brains necessary to make handaxes, Palaeolithic people did not make a wide range of tools. Sharp-edged flakes that had been removed in the production of axes were undoubtedly used as knives, and other flakes were retouched along an edge, or notched, and used to scrape leather, bone or wood. Some groups used only flake tools which have traditionally been described as Clactonian after the type was found at Clacton-on-Sea

in Essex in about 1911. No one knows whether the people who made them were different from other groups or whether these variations are the result of the availability of good flint, the climate or just choice. The debate continues amongst archaeologists although it is now accepted that Clactonian tools are not earlier than Acheulian handaxes, which was once thought to be the case.

Handaxes remained virtually unchanged in design for the next 450,000 years. Towards the end of that period a specialized technique for flaking flint – the Levallois technique, after the Paris suburb where it was first recorded – was developed to make scrapers, knives and spear points.

Homo Sapiens arrived in Britain during the Upper Palaeolithic period, about 40,000 years ago, and introduced an entirely new form of flint technology to the Levallois technique which involved the production of long, slender, parallel-sided pieces of flint called blades. Its most important features were that it was the most economic way of creating a cutting edge, that it produced a standardized end product and that it enabled a wider range of tools to be made than had ever been possible before. Archaeologists have discovered that, as a result of this new technology, piercers, engraving tools and arrow points were added to the scrapers, knives and spear points produced by the Levallois technique, many of which were by now glued into wooden handles.

The Upper Palaeolithic is poorly represented in the British Isles, probably because it coincided with the last glaciation. However, a skeleton dated to 27,000 years ago was found in a cave in Paviland in south Wales which shows that people did visit Britain then, probably during short spells of warmer weather.

Recolonization of Britain began in earnest about 12,000 years ago and people from this period, some of whom lived in caves in Cheddar Gorge, Somerset – one of these, Cooper's Hole, was the subject of a *Time Team* investigation – continued to make blade tools, though the size of the tools decreased.

The beginning of the present interglacial is connected with the last groups of hunters who lived in Britain before the introduction of agriculture. The tools these Mesolithic (Middle Stone Age) people produced were similar to those made by their Upper Palaeolithic predecessors – but they eventually became much smaller and are called microliths (small stones). Our Mesolithic ancestors were also responsible for introducing the shafted woodworking axe.

Mammoth Teeth

Mammoths were large elephants with long, dramatically curved tusks. They ranged over most of Europe, northern and central Asia and North America, and their remains are commonly found as fossils in deposits in caves and rivers. They became highly specialized grass-eating grazers, and this specialization can be seen in the structure of their cheek teeth. Each tooth is made up of a series of thin plates of hard dental enamel, dentine and relatively soft dental cement that are firmly cemented together to form a brick-like block. As the teeth wore down with use, the different hardnesses of the plates created and maintained strong transverse ridges on the biting surfaces, which were used to shear up the grasses and other low-growing vegetation on which mammoths fed – a bit like giant lawnmowers.

During its lifetime a mammoth could grow, and wear down, six cheek teeth in each side of its jaw, both top and bottom – like today's elephants. The first tooth in each jaw is tiny; the last one is huge! At any one time only one or two teeth in each half-jaw would be in the process of being worn down; new teeth formed at the back of the jaw and moved forward to replace the ones in front that had been worn away. It is possible to see an evolutionary trend in the pattern of mammoths' teeth: as the animals changed from a leaf-eating to a grass-eating way of life the crowns became higher and the number of plates in each tooth increased. The size and shape of the mammoth teeth at Stanton Harcourt in Oxfordshire helped *Time Team* to date the site to a temperate period about 200,000 to 170,000 years ago.

experimental archaeology

Experimental archaeology – replicating past technologies and tools and finding out how they functioned – allows us to test theories that for years have been expounded in print as gospel truth. One of the first people to practise this branch of archaeology was Sir John Evans who, at the end of the nineteenth century, demonstrated to an international conference in Norwich that it was possible to make stone tools with stone and antler hammers.

Serious scientific experiments have been conducted since then, on almost every period, material and object, and experimental archaeology is now seen as a branch of study in its own right. Experiments are rigorously thought out, justified and planned, taking into account what is known from excavations and information about the level of technology that may have been available at the time, so that archaeologists know what they are likely to reveal. It is unlikely that the results will tell precisely how something was done; rather they will suggest how it might have been done. Some experiments are fairly short term, intended to answer simple questions; others, for example to test how a bank and ditch erode and silt up, may continue for over 100 years with frequent monitoring.

On sites, it is the broken and failed pieces discarded during manufacture that interest an experimental archaeologist, as they provide the best information about how objects should have been made – finished pieces are often devoid of traces of manufacture. Experiments involving organic objects are difficult because remains of these rarely survive on sites.

By making handaxes such as this one he made at Elveden, Suffolk, Phil has learnt much about the skills of our palaeolithic ancestors

Many *Time Team* cameos have involved real experimental archaeology and the experts who demonstrate, or advise on, a particular skill have often been put on the spot when asked to perform a task using authentic tools, rather than their own modern equivalents. Using honeysuckle to make the tow rope at Seahenge was just one example of this. Making objects by hand is a recurring theme in these experiments and demonstrates the length of time it took to perform certain skills before power tools were available. Sometimes, it also allows the modern craftsman to get into the mind of his ancient predecessor, to feel the anguish at mistakes and imagine the joy at a job well done. The downside of experimental archaeology is that it has to be recorded and the results must be published for the work to have any real value.

pollen analysis

Pollen grains are produced by all plant species – a process that, as sufferers from hay fever know, reaches a peak a certain times of the year – and these male 'seeds' are released to fertilize females. Many of them never make it and fall to the ground where they either rot or are eaten. However, in certain circumstances – if they fall on a bog or into a lake, for example – they may become waterlogged and be preserved for immense periods of time.

pollen grains being analysed under the microscope by environmental archaeologists at Stanton Harcourt

Pollen analysis was developed first in Denmark in 1956, and then at Cambridge University by Professor Harry Godwin and his students. They found that by taking sections through peat beds and bogs and looking at the preserved pollen, it was possible to build build up a picture of what a landscape had been like in the past – open grassland during one period, heavily forested at another. At the time they were unable to date the phases of vegetation but this can now be done using radiocarbon dating.

Not all trees, shrubs and grasses produce the same amount of pollen – there is less from oaks, for example – and because the grains are different sizes not all of them travel the same distance. The heaviest fall nearby while the wind may carry lighter ones for many kilometres. Pollen analysts have to allow for these variations. Each species of pollen is different and even when the grains have broken up, most of them can be readily identified. Nevertheless, analyzing the pollen in a section of peat, dating the various layers and describing the vegetation and the way it has changed through time requires a great deal of skill.

Over the years pollen analysis has revealed how the original 'wildwood' of Britain was dominated by lime, hornbeam and oak, but also contained all the trees we are familiar with today. This woodland had developed from tundra after the last glaciation and gone through a cool temperate phase of birch, pine and juniper before becoming full forest. Successive phases of clearance by prehistoric people have also been revealed. These begin with the Mesolithic period and then the clearance and revegetation of the Neolithic. Finally, in the Bronze Age (on chalk uplands) and the Iron Age (in major river valleys) woodland was fully cleared to create an open landscape.

Phil on...the Palaeolithic

The Palaeolithic is my favourite period because it's so old, so long ago. It is what made me interested in archaeology. It's where we came from. If our Stone Age ancestors hadn't made it through evolution, we wouldn't be here now! They had to make all the initial discoveries. It's an amazing time.

There is nothing like picking up a handaxe. It is the only sort of connection you're ever going to have with the person who made it and it still gives me a tingle. I specifically remember one I found in Kent. The site was a vast gravel quarry and although a few handaxes had been found on the spoil heap there was nothing in situ. I was wandering through the pit and walked up to the gravel face and picked out a stone – it was a handaxe. It was the one and only time I have ever found one like that. There's less chance of that happening than winning the Lottery.

Everyone associates the Palaeolithic period with the cave man, but there aren't very many caves in Britain. Most of them are in limestone regions like the Mendips in Somerset and the Derbyshire peaks, and in a few other upland areas, yet most palaeoliths are actually found in areas where there are no caves. So the idea of the cave man is a bit of a misnomer. Although it's very nice to think about him and how he lived in caves, basically he didn't!

From the Wash to the Severn – the classic definition of southern Britain – is the area that yields the most handaxes, and yet there are very few caves in this lowland landscape. Palaeolithic people would probably have lived in temporary shelters of some kind and presumably used organic stuff, like grasses or leather, to make them.

Most of the sites we know about are in deposits of gravel laid down by a river next to which people would have been living. In Palaeolithic times the river would have been a great, powerful torrent and tools would just fall into it and be carried away. Sometimes you get a late twentieth-century gravel pit like Boxgrove in West Sussex where there are loads of handaxes. Other times, an axe can just pop up totally unexpectedly. At the Roman site we were digging in Lower Basildon, Berkshire, a handaxe turned up on the spoil heap – I was as sick as a parrot when someone else found it!

Although you get fewer finds in the Palaeolithic, it means that when you do uncover something the memory of that moment really sticks with you. Your twenty-seventh bucketful of everyday Roman pottery is hardly different from your twenty-sixth one and you'll scarcely remember it. But if you find a flint, that stays with you for years and years. If that is the piece that dates the site, it doesn't matter how grubby it is, you go home with a big smile on your face!

One of the nicest, most memorable things I've found was from the Upper Palaeolithic – about 12,000 years ago. It was an antler harpoon from a rock shelter in the Dordogne Valley in southwest France. That was a glorious, beautiful piece, and particularly special because it was the one thing we wanted to find. We dined out on champagne that evening – the director of the excavation had promised it to anybody who found a piece of art, and if that wasn't a piece of art I don't know what was!

faunal analysis

A variety of animals existed in Britain in the Upper Palaeolithic period (500,000–11,000 years ago) – mammoth, elephant, lion, bear, bison, hyena and horse. The first task of a palaeozoologist faced with a collection of bones from an archaeological site is identifying the animals the bones are from. Those that are very common can be identified at a glance. For others, however, including rarer species, or species such as donkeys and ponies that look quite similar, the archaeological bones are identified by comparing them with bones from known animals. Large archaeological institutions and universities have macabre collections of skeletons of all shapes and sizes against which excavated bones can be compared. In the case of animals that still exist, most of the skeletons come from animals that died recently – someone may have had the unpleasant task of boiling up a dead rat, sheep or bison in acid to remove its flesh and leave the bones clean so the skeleton could be reassembled. In the case of extinct animals such as mammoths, bones have to be identified using rarer comparatives, mostly in museums.

Once the species has been identified, the palaeozoologist starts to look for more detailed information. Bones and teeth both provide evidence for the age at which the animal died. The size of the former is a good guide, of course, but if the ends of limb bones are not firmly attached to the main shaft of the limb bone, it shows that the animal was still growing and died before it was fully adult. Teeth also provide good clues – some mammals have a set of 'milk teeth' which are replaced at the end of infancy, so if these are present it means the animal was very young when it died. On the other hand, very worn teeth usually suggest that an animal lived to an old age.

Sex is more difficult to identify. In many animals females are smaller than males, and if there are a lot of bones the larger and smaller ones can be grouped separately. However, this will only give a tentative indication of how many males and females there are. DNA analysis can identify the sex of an animal for certain, but the technique is expensive, so it is rarely practical to use it on a large scale.

If a lot of bones have been found, a palaeozoologist will try and estimate the number of animals – which is not as easy as it might seem at first glance. The problem is that if there are 100 different bones from the same species of animal it is impossible to know whether they represent a near-complete single skeleton, or one bone from each of 100 animals. Counting the number of bones that each animal has only one of (the lower jaw, for example) will provide an estimate of how many animals there are – there must have been at least one for every jaw – but this may be far too low because the jaws from some animals may be missing. The only solution is to count several different bones, and assume that the true number lies somewhere between the highest and lowest totals.

A palaeozoologist will also look for marks on the bones. Breaks, holes or scours may be the result of damage by weapons, perhaps when the animal was hunted. Finer cut marks may show that it was butchered for food – the position of these can even tell us exactly how the meat was portioned up. Some diseases and dietary deficiencies can also leave telltale marks on bone. All this information is useful, not only because it tells us the kind of animals that were around in the past, but because it also tells us about the way humans used them. A well-preserved bone, even one from nearly half a million years ago, can reveal whether an animal had been eaten by humans, whether it had been actively hunted or just scavenged (or, in later periods, kept in captivity as domestic livestock), and whether it was only young, sick or old animals that were picked off or if humans were confident enough to choose an animal in its prime as prey.

A variety of animal bones from the palaeolithic period found at stanton Harcourt, including a number of large mammoth teeth

biological analysis

A whole range of techniques is available to analyse biological material. One of these, the study of phytoliths and diatoms, can help with reconstructing the environment at a particular time. Phytoliths are minute particles of silica from plant cells which remain after the plant has been eaten or has decomposed or been burnt. Diatoms are small single-celled algae with silica cell walls. Different species indicate different water conditions and the technique – which is very specialised – is similar to pollen analysis.

Perhaps more useful, and certainly more easy, is studying larger fragments of plants such as seeds, grains and pips (some of which may be carbonized), leaves, twigs and pieces of wood. These are usually collected using some sort of 'flotation' device where samples are sieved and lighter material is floated off and collected.

The cereal grains, seeds and fruit pips indicate the food people were eating, while leaves, twigs and and wood reveal the kinds of trees, bushes and shrubs that were growing locally.

seeds and grains being sieved for biological analysis at finlaggan

Mick on... Palaeolithic sites

I always think about Elveden in Suffolk when I look back on the Palaeolithic sites *Time Team* has excavated. It dates to about 400,000 BC when it was part of a system of rivers or palaeochannels , and we knew that Stone Age men and women had been there because bones and flint tools that had been washed along by the water have been found in silt deposited by these ancient waterways. Elveden also has a lot of animal and insect remains and through environmental sampling we were able to examine these and build up a picture of the animals that would have inhabited the landscape.

For me, one of the most striking moments of the excavation was when Stewart Ainsworth and I flew over the site in a helicopter. Stewart had maps showing the location of former river courses that had been revealed when Victorian brick-makers dug a vast pit in their search for clay. I realised that I was looking at a landscape that is basically postglacial and dates from 13,000 BC onwards. Yet the site we were digging, and all the material Stewart was trying to sort out, related to something that was ten times older. We were looking for a landscape that had been totally obliterated, and, in fact, literally turned around the entire drainage pattern, which had gone in one direction in the Palaeolithic and was now going in the opposite one. It is impossible to comprehend something like this. So in landscape terms

the Palaeolithic is a closed door. You can only look through the keyholes that archaeologists, geologists or quarrymen have made and say, 'Look down there.' The programme at Stanton Harcourt in Oxfordshire was the same. There again, although the site was 200,000 years more recent then Elveden, it was still 200,000 years old. I find it difficult to relate to such distant periods because my interests and training are concerned with existing landscape – and what was there in the Palaeolithic was wiped away by glaciers. There are some palaeochannels in the illustration of Palaeolithic Timechester and they're still there up to the Bronze Age.

If I had to live in one particular prehistoric period I would go for the Mesolithic – about 8,000 years ago, between the Palaeolithic and the Neolithic – because, according to arguments put forward by anthropologists and archaeologists, anyone who survived childhood had a relatively easy life in what was a hunter-gatherer society. Marshall Sahlins has studied modern hunter-gatherers who have been driven to the margins of regions because the best areas are occupied by farmers. His analysis revealed that they spend most of the time sleeping. 'Food procurement' comes way down on the list. So it seems probable that, like their modern descendants, Mesolithic people knew exactly where they were in their landscape, where they would find roots and leaves and when nuts and berries would ripen. They were able to track animals and knew the migration routes of horse and antelope. It might have been difficult to kill a mammoth, but its meat wasn' t an essential part of their prehistoric diet: the staples were roots, leaves and berries, small mammals, eggs and shellfish. We can see this from sites like Elveden and Stanton Harcourt where large-scale environmental sampling has revealed the range of food that was available to Stone Age people.

neolithic

carenza's story of
Timechester in 3,000 BC

In 3,000 BC Timechester has changed out of all recognition. It is still a largely wooded landscape divided by a river, but the river follows a different course and the trees are different species. The herds of mammoths and elephants have vanished, and because the sea level has risen a coastline, dotted with small semipermanent settlements, is visible on the horizon. A few small open spaces have appeared in the forested landscape and in some of them there are small stands of cereals or a cluster of huts with pens for pigs or cattle. On one hilltop there is a clearing containing a long low structure of huge stones with a dark entrance at one end, while on another people are gathered near a series of small curving ditches which together make up a vast circular enclosure. But there is little other evidence of human impact on the landscape. Why has Timechester changed so much – and yet so little – over nearly half a million years?

The greatest changes since 450,000 BC have had little or nothing to do with human intervention. It was the ice sheets repeatedly advancing and retreating over thousands of years that scoured the landscape and changed the shape of the hills and the course of the river. For hundreds of thousands of years Timechester saw only brief flashes of human activity which left little or no lasting trace beyond an occasional handful of discarded stone tools.

A quarter of a million years after the first visitors left Timechester, *Homo Erectus* had become extinct and a new species of human had camped in the area for a few days. Like their predecessors, these Neanderthal people (named after the region in Germany where their bones were first found) were hunters and gatherers who went where their natural food sources took them and did not stay long in any one place. But they were taller and more heavily built than the earlier humans and had bigger brains contained by skulls with larger, rounded foreheads. They could design and create new tools from flakes of flint which they, like *Homo Erectus*, left

behind them as they strayed across the valley in pursuit of food.

After a further 200,000 years or so another new group of humans arrived for the first time at Timechester. Just as the Neanderthals had replaced *Homo Erectus*, so they replaced the Neanderthals. *Homo Sapiens* was genetically identical to modern men and women. During a short warmer period between two ice ages a family group sheltered for a winter in a small cave overlooking the Time Valley. They hunted mainly horses, whose meat they could eat and whose hides they could wear by sewing them together with needles made from slivers of the animals' bones. Aware of their dependence on horses, they carved delicate images of them on discarded ribs to bring luck in future hunts. In the cold, barren landscape the shelter they had found in the valley was not to be forgotten, and they returned to the cave each winter to live in its entrance. When one of the group died they did as they had done for generations. They used thin parallel-sided blades

of flint to diligently skin, disembowel and dismember the body and remove the tongue, then placed the remains respectfully in the deeper recesses of the cave.

Scores of generations of seasonal occupation of the cave ended in about 8,800 BC, when the temperature dropped sharply causing the ice sheets to advance once again. When humans next came to the Time Valley 800 years later they spurned the cave in favour of a spot on the edge of a new marshy, reed-fringed lake. This early Mesolithic, or Middle Stone Age, landscape was still only thinly scattered with birch and pine trees and there were fewer big herd animals to be hunted. But fish, birds and small mammals were in plentiful supply by the lakeside, and were easily caught from small canoes with the help of new sophisticated barbed harpoons made from bone or antler. Roots, shoots, berries and nuts amply supplemented this diet and sustained those who worked hard processing antlers and tanning hides. Eventually the group moved to another site, near the sea whose tides seemed to rise higher each year.

Over tens of generations hazel, oak, lime and elm trees appeared in an increasingly thickly wooded landscape, as did greater numbers of larger mammals including deer and wild pigs. But the animals were wary, and had to be carefully stalked by any group that reoccupied the lakeside spot long after its Mesolithic use had been forgotten. To increase their chances of success, hunters wore disguises including headdresses fashioned from deer skulls complete with horns. The bead necklaces made from pebble and shale that these humans usually wore had to be removed lest they rattle and alert the intended prey.

Many centuries passed before the first permanent structures were built in the valley in about 4,000 BC. By this time it was occupied by the same small family groups who moved seasonally from summer to winter settlements. The more sedentary regime suited these Neolithic people: more babies were born and fewer children died. Older people, spared the strain of constant migration, lived longer and passed on their skills and knowledge of the solutions to problems. When a lean time came it was they who remembered where other sources of food had been found in previous bad years a generation or so before, and saved the group from starvation. Slowly, the population began to rise.

In 3,000 BC, the Time Valley was their land. Their ancestors lay in the huge stone-chambered tomb that stood proudly on the skyline, visible to anyone entering the valley. Its small chambers formed a long barrow and contained the selected bones of chosen individuals, placed there reverently once the flesh had fallen away. Around 3,000 BC, a young woman had died and gone to join her ancestors after her body had lain for four seasons on the top of a nearby hill where, to mark her passing, the group had dug a short section of ditch. This was customary when anyone died and the section was one of many ditches that now made a complete circular causewayed enclosure around the hilltop where she had lain for a year. When they came to take her bones away and place them in the long barrow, the feasting and dancing in the hilltop enclosure had lasted for three days. The rubbish that resulted was placed carefully in 'her' section of ditch.

A cow from the herd that never strayed far from the open grassy areas occupied by settlements or monuments had been killed for the feast; and chosen people from distant valleys had walked for seven days or more to join the celebration. As was the custom, gifts were exchanged. The occupants of the Time Valley gave their visitors polished stone axes, each of which had taken days to chip into shape and rub completely smooth. They, in their turn, received seeds. It was said that if these were put in cleared ground the land would bear grass-like plants which would, in a year's time, produce ten times the number of similar seeds, which could be eaten, kept and sown. The Time Valley group was sceptical, but a gift given in these circumstances could not be spurned, so the seeds had duly been planted.

The entrance to cooper's hole, cheddar — during neolithic times the entrances to caves provided shelter during the colder months

fieldwalking

F ieldwalking is one of the most useful ways of finding out where to dig on a site. It is also a relaxing way to spend a morning or afternoon, with the added excitement of uncovering items before starting excavations. The most common types of material that are found are well-fired pottery, roof tiles and flints, which are all dateable and survive extensive ploughing. Objects from a range of periods may be found.

A properly laid-out grid is necessary so that finds can be located and plotted accurately at a later stage. Garden canes, with taped ends to make them visible, are used to mark its corners and it can be displayed on the relevant section of the Ordnance Survey national grid for convenience.

There are two basic types of fieldwalking: line walking and total collection. The first involves teams walking across a field along parallel lines that are at equal distances from each other – usually about 20 to 25 metres (65 to 82 feet), although they may be closer. 'Finds bags' are labelled with an appropriate site code and grid reference and are changed at 20 to 25 metre (65 to 82 feet) intervals to establish how objects are distributed on the grid. Line walking is useful for fairly rapid assessment surveys across quite large areas and for detecting broad patterns of archaeological activity. It can also be used to sample a dense concentration of material where it would be impractical to collect every find on the surface. Total collection involves collecting everything from a 1 metre or 10 metre (3 or 32 foot) grid square. It is the more detailed of the two methods and may be used as a follow-up to line walking.

Each survey is accompanied by copious written records. It is necessary to know whether there are significant slopes which may have moved finds downhill. As fieldwalking is generally done between the autumn and spring, after crops have been harvested and before new ones obscure visibility, it is important to know how much crop growth is present so that any impairment to visibility that might bias the results is noted. Fields should be allowed to weather before they are examined as this increases the chances that rain will have washed surface mud from finds and make them easier to see. However, it is sometimes necessary to walk a field when it is freshly cultivated and this may influence the amount of material recovered; if this is the case, it is noted in the records. The winter sun casts long shadows which make it difficult to see objects in the ground. Even if all the walkers in a team are experienced, comparisons of their results often reveal different levels of ability or a preference for finds of a particular type.

The most difficult aspect of fieldwalking is ensuring that everyone proceeds at the same pace. Some people rush across a field finding only the large obvious pieces, while others dawdle, picking up everything they see, and often stray off their line in the process. The most rewarding part is calculating the results and plotting the distribution of material to provide a general guide to how objects are distributed in an area. A dense concentration of finds from a single period is likely to indicate the presence of a site that is worth excavating, while dispersed concentrations may just represent material that has been thrown out with manure and spread through ploughing.

Neolithic Axes

Polished stone axes were used for woodworking, forest clearance and even weapons during the Neolithic period, and are also thought to have been of symbolic importance. Most of them were made by pecking – literally pounding – one stone with another to make the shape of an axe. However, given a suitable stone, a hammer (also made of stone) could be used to flake pieces off instead. The flaking method was the more manageable of the two, but whichever one was used, the axe was then ground down with another stone to get a polished finish – a time-consuming task that would not have been undertaken without good reason.

The advantages of a polished axe were, first, that it was a beautiful object and therefore valuable as an item of trade and exchange; and, second, that it was more functional than an unpolished one: grinding removed all the irregularities that created weak points – areas where the stone could crack or split – within the blade and body of the axe. In addition, grinding the blade created one continuous, strong cutting edge.

Once the axe had been polished it was hafted, or bound, to a wooden handle with plant fibres, leather thongs or animal gut.

global positioning by satellite

This small screen displays information about Time Team's position

One of the ironies of archaeology is that the very modern equipment that is used is so often in contrast with the very old sites that are being studied. There can be no greater anachronism than using a global positioning by satellite (GPS) system to locate ones from the Stone Age – twenty-first-century space-age technology recording the dawn of humankind in Britain! GPS is the name for a constellation of American satellites in orbit around the earth. Archaeologists use these to locate – well, anything – very accurately. Both the United States and Russia developed the technology during the Cold War as part of military spying, communications and defence systems. However, information from the satellites can now be used for peaceful purposes, including archaeology. In Britain we use the American system (nick-named 'Star Wars').

A GPS consists of a base station, which consists of a radio and an antenna, a second radio and a movable piece of kit called a 'rover', which is used to do the actual measuring. Before starting, it is necessary to find out if enough satellites are switched on to tell you where you are – there must be at least four, and more is better. Not all are in view at the same time, so the first step is to ask the computer's 'almanac' when the required number of satellites will be in the relevant area – if there aren't enough of them at any point, you will lose 'lock' and be unable to do any more measuring until some are back in sight. It sounds risky, but the worst problem is actually trees and buildings that can block the signal.

When enough satellites are in position the base station is set up, anywhere on the site. The next step is to use the second radio to visit three 'trig points' (two will do, but three make for a more accurate reading). These points are little concrete pyramids located by the Ordnance Survey – there is a network of them right across the country – marked on all the organization's maps. However, the exact coordinate information has to be bought from them. At each of the three trig points the radio is set up to receive a signal from all the satellites within range. Once this has been done (quite hard work as the points are usually several miles apart and not always accessible by road) the GPS system knows exactly where the on-site base station is in relation to the satellites and on the Ordnance Survey national grid map for Britain – all to an accuracy of a couple of millimetres.

After some computer processing to set up the site grid and insert the 'trig points' the rover is switched on and used to go to any point and locate it on a plan of the site. GPS can establish the point's coordinates, show its position on a map, lay out a grid and a myriad other things – it can even find a point that has been previously measured and guide you back to it. It is very quick, very accurate and the only reason every archaeological dig doesn't use it is that it is also very expensive.

opposite: Bernard's bit of kit! The base station for the GPS system, with Bernard holding the staff

Phil on... the Neolithic

Thank God the Neolithic is still in the Stone Age, with no metal contaminants! I do like digging Neolithic sites. In fact, one of my all-time favourite sites was from this period, and that was Grimes Grave, a famous flint-mine site in Norfolk. For someone as obsessed about flint as I am, the opportunity to spend five years digging there was something like heaven. Just clambering around in those underground galleries and seeing how they worked was wonderful. I remember the antler picks that the Neolithic miners used to take out the chalk. Sometimes their hands got all covered in chalky clay, then they'd lift their pick up leaving clay on the handle, and you could still see their handprints in the clay.

We dug this shaft – in those days, people didn't bother about health and safety anywhere near as much as they do today – and it horrifies me to think about it now. It must have been absolutely lethal, but once we were knew we were in this virgin pit we just had to go for it, digging down and down and down. It was that spirit of adventure, we had to keep digging. I remember I clambered into a gallery and took all the chalk out. The far end was totally empty and there were bone wedges in there used by the miners to break up the chalk walls and axe marks because they'd used stone axes to carve the gallery out. I thought to myself, 'Nobody's

been in this gallery for 4,000 years.' I was the first person in there for 4,000 years. It was just absolutely incredible, absolutely incredible.

Another place I associate with the Neolithic is Amesbury, at one end of the Stonehenge cursus, where I dug out a ditch that went alongside a long barrow. Some time later word reached me that some flint-knapping debris had actually been found there. So I hopped on my pushbike and went hurtling along the track back to the site, and sure enough at the bottom of the ditch I saw a little cluster of flints.

It turned out that this was undoubtedly where somebody had actually knapped the flint. I could work out where he'd done this. He'd had three different bits of flint and it was possible to piece together the sequence in which the lumps were worked. I collected all the flints, stuck them back together again and there was one minute little core missing. There was not even one flake missing – just the core. He hadn't made any tools at all, he just sat there and knapped. Whoever knapped that flint liked flint knapping, just like me. I knap flint for some pretty inane reasons at times, I just like doing it. Maybe that person was exactly the same. To me, it was something he'd done during his dinner break. He was digging out this ditch and he found a nice piece of flint and thought, 'Oh that looks all right. I might see how that goes'.

Neolithic settlement sites are very rare in Britain. In the north, you've got Skara Brae and its houses in the Orkneys, but trying to piece a settlement together in the south is very difficult. There are henge monuments, flint mines and barrows, and then there are just pits. I'm not sure whether pits, if you can find them, make very good television. So *Time Team* hasn't really focused on sites from this period. It was therefore really nice when we found a Neolithic mortuary enclosure at Basildon in Lower Berkshire.

Neolithic Pottery

The beginning of the Neolithic period in Britain – about 4,000 BC – is defined as the point at which pottery was first used. The remains found on archaeological sites are usually broken sherds of dark, chunky, fired clay that can look deceptively like dried mud – but are a lot harder. Large fragments of stone or shell, sometimes as much as 4 or 5 millimetres (about ¼ inch) across, are visible in the broken sides of the sherds and were added to the clay to prevent the pot breaking up during firing. This was done in a clamp kiln – a bonfire set in a pit and covered with turf. Although ordinary bonfires were sometimes used for firing, they did not reach the high temperatures necessary to produce strong, durable pots.

The pots were made by coiling long snakes of clay in a rising spiral and then smoothing over the joints, and could be anything from a few centimetres (about 1 to 1½ inches) to about 40 centimetres (15 inches) high. Many were plain with no kind of ornamentation, especially in the earlier Neolithic period, but as time passed more and more pots were decorated with scratched lines, herringbone patterns, fingertip impressions or stuck-on strips of clay. Other designs were made by pressing grains or ears of wheat against the unfired pot. Cords of plant fibres or animal gut or skin were also used to make patterns, providing us with almost the only evidence that they were made in Britain during the later Neolithic period. Presumably they were also used for clothes and to construct hide tents.

Domestic settlement sites are the main sources of Neolithic pottery, and the remains found in these can tell us something about how the houses of the period were furnished. Early vessels had rounded bases, like the ones in Victor's drawing which are being dried out before being fired, which meant they were made to sit on a rough surface such as the ground. Later ones, however, had flat bases suitable for standing on a flat surface, which suggests that people were starting to build and use domestic furniture like shelves and cupboards.

radiocarbon dating

All living things contain normal carbon-12 and small proportions of radioactive carbon-13 and -14. The latter are produced by cosmic radiation and are found in the upper atmosphere, but all kinds of carbon get into plants as carbon dioxide and then into animals when they eat the plants and/or other animals. The proportion of carbon-14 is constantly topped up as food is taken in and remains constant until the plant or animal dies.

Carbon-14 begins to decay after death because it is not being replenished, and it has been found that only half is left after 5,730 years (the 'half-life'). After a further 5,370 years only half of this (a quarter of the original amount) remains. It is possible to trace carbon-14 back to about 70,000 years, after which quantities are too small to be measured.

Willand Libby of Chicago discovered the process in 1946 and it was not long before its potential for absolute dating of archaeological finds was realized.

Throughout the 1960s and 1970s it was used for former living material that contained carbon. Any date that was quoted had a statistical probability applied, usually something like '250 BC + or − 50', meaning that there was a 66 per cent probability that it lay somewhere between 300 and 200 BC. In this example a 98 per cent probability, might result in a date between 350 and 150 BC. Many radiocarbon dates were therefore not very precise, something that is often forgotten when they are quoted. Nevertheless, carbon-14 dating was much more accurate than relative dating, which had previously been all that was possible.

Research into dendrochronology – the information contained in tree rings, which can give a precise date – eventually showed that the further back we go, the further carbon-14 dates were from actual dates. For example, by 5,000 BC, when a carbon-14 sample should have been showing an age of 7,000 years, the dates it indicated were centred on 6,000 BC – 1,000 years too young. There are various complex reasons for this. In addition, the line of carbon-14 dates and their relation to actual dates shown by dendrochronology is not even – some alarming wiggles make it difficult to date samples in, for example, the Iron Age. It is possible to get round this by obtaining dates from more samples and 'wiggle watching' them against the curve.

A lot of progress has been made since the 1980s with the introduction of accelerator mass spectrometry (AMS). This counts the different atoms of carbon-12, carbon-13 and carbon-14 and, in so doing, gives much more accurate dates from much smaller samples. AMS labs have produced some surprising results from both early human remains and fragments of rare and valuable objects such as the Turin Shroud.

Although radiocarbon dates are not as accurate as the best dendrochronology ones, the technique has revolutionized archaeology in the last fifty years. Previously there had been no way of getting near an 'absolute' date for finds and sites – and relative dating, and many ideas associated with it, was wildly inaccurate. Attempting to date archaeological material is no longer the agonizing problem it once was.

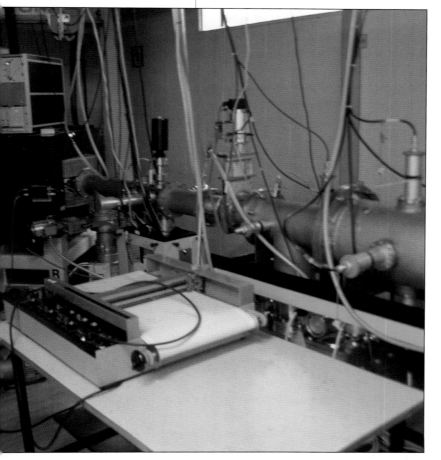

part of the equipment used in the accelerator mass spectrometry process in the main lab at oxford

The story of Timechester highlights periods that *Time Team* has not yet investigated, and of these the one that stands out most is the Neolithic. However, we have uncovered objects from this time when excavating other sites – although each programme tends to be focused on a particular dominant period we often find items from different ones. For example, we found a Neolithic mortuary enclosure at Lower Basildon in Berkshire even though the main site was Roman. And at Navan in County Armagh, where the aim of the excavation was to find evidence for pagan and Christian activities, we uncovered a lovely polished stone axe from the Neolithic. So this period has crept into a couple of programmes.

The key question about the Neolithic is: why would anybody want to develop agriculture? Why would people choose to adopt a lifestyle that was different to the Mesolithic one described in the last chapter? Farming is hard work, and there's no time to doze under a tree or sit around telling stories. To my mind, its development was connected with population growth. Whether our Neolithic predecessors began farming because this would make it possible to support more people in the future, or whether they took the idea on board – from other societies that practised agriculture – because the population was already increasing and more food was needed, is not clear. My view is that its adoption was the result of the latter: the landscape can only support a certain number of hunter-gatherers and I think agriculture probably developed in the Neolithic period because more children were surviving the early years of childhood and people were living longer. Unfortunately the archaeological evidence for this is very slim.

Another characteristic of Neolithic societies is that they did what no one had ever done before: they built monuments. As far as we can tell, hunter-gatherers didn't do this, but the early farmers built burial chambers to start with, then causewayed enclosures and other monumental structures.

It would be pure luck to get glimpses of the Neolithic at Timechester or any other similar site because there were no urban centres, just small, rural settlements which are easy to miss – and so much from the period has been covered by later developments. One of these glimpses came from medieval London when development work along the Strand turned up an extremely high density of Neolithic axes. The reason they were there is nothing to do with the Neolithic period – rather, they came from the Middle Ages when they were thought to be thunderbolts and wealthy people put them in their roofs to prevent their houses being struck by lightning. So finding a Neolithic axe in a medieval city probably doesn't mean quite what it might seem to suggest. However, at Dorchester in Dorset archaeologists dug through the medieval and Roman parts of the town and uncovered some big pits. They were going to leave them, but a digger continued excavating at lunchtime and found that one of them was a huge Neolithic pit. They had uncovered part of a henge monument or big timber circle. This kind of discovery is totally unpredictable. It is possible to make a certain number of predictions about what a town excavation will reveal and what the dates of the finds are likely to be, but what was there before the town is anybody's guess.

CHAPTER 3
bronze age

carenza's story of Timechester in 1,500 BC

Another 1,500 years have passed and for the first time in the history of Timechester the results of earlier human actions are visible in the later landscape. In 1,500 BC the slight traces of the Neolithic causewayed enclosure are still apparent as grassy hollows in the ground, but the site is now just used as a landmark for dividing up settlement territories. The massive, stone-chambered tomb has been covered with earth and is now a huge grassy mound. It is still the most dominant monument, standing proud on the skyline and, although it is no longer used to house the bones of the dead, the tomb has become the focus of a new style of burial – underneath smaller round barrows. But in the foreground a different funerary rite is being carried out: bodies are left in the open on a wooden platform hidden in the marsh, to rot and be picked clean by birds and animals. A little way away, grassy banks indicate the presence of a henge. Made up of a circle of standing timber posts surrounded by a low ditch and inner bank, it has been built, used for worship and abandoned in the 1,500 years since our last look at Timechester. By no means everything from the Neolithic period has left its trace. There is no sign of the earlier settlement, which is now overlain by small paddocks and animal pens. The present settlement, like its predecessor, occupies a prime site in the Time Valley on dry, raised ground near the river. The heavily wooded landscape has been partly cleared to make way for fields around each of the increasingly numerous small, permanent settlements that are scattered around the landscape. How have these changes happened?

The seeds that were first planted at Timechester in 3,000 BC did indeed grow, and although tending them was hard work, they provided a healthy crop of Emmer wheat. This was stored and during the winter the contents of all but two bags were ground up to make gruel and rough bread. Although this was by no means the only food

– even during winter the valley's occupants continued to hunt animals and collect plants – everyone agreed that the security of knowing that the wheat was there, ready to provide a sustaining meal if all else failed, made the hard work of tending it worthwhile.

The seeds in two bags of uneaten grain were resown in the spring, establishing a cycle that would be repeated again and again. Over many generations the yields grew gradually larger, as more wheat was harvested each year, allowing more seeds to be kept for resowing. The small patch of sown ground grew steadily larger and other crops including miniature barley were also introduced. Children and the infirm, unable to go out to forage or hunt, watched over it. They scared off birds that would otherwise eat the newly planted seeds and kept away wandering sheep, cows or horses that would have enjoyed the tender young shoots of the newly sprouting grain. Whereas the settlement had previously been abandoned from season to season as the group followed herds of cows or goats

into higher ground or went to fish by the coast, there was now always someone living at the settlement to tend and guard the wheat.

The important role that wheat played in the life of the settlement seemed

to require the courting of new gods. Stories told at the feasts that were held each year after harvest described how to do this. Accordingly, a new monument was built on lower ground: an enclosed ground space defined by an earthen bank with an outer ditch. The belief was that walking around the circular shape of this henge would ensure that the harvest season always came round again, while the ditch and bank would prevent the good fortune needed for a good harvest from escaping. One by one, huge timber posts made from tree trunks were stood on end inside the circle to represent standing stalks of wheat, their bases wedged in huge pits and held steady by large stones. But only a few people knew what rites went on inside the henge; the ceremonies were hidden from the view of most of the people of Timechester by the massive bank.

One day, while chasing away a small group of wild sheep, two strong young children managed to catch a particularly persistent offender and bring it triumphantly into the settlement, still alive. A surplus of meat from a hunt made slaughtering the sheep unnecessary, so it was suggested that

Emmer wheat growing in Mick's back garden

the best way to keep it off the crop was to tether it. This would allow its milk to be taken every day and its fleece could be plucked for wool. Given a handful of wheat, the sheep soon settled down. Within a few years, the humans had trapped and bred a small herd of sheep and goats and a handful of cows, for which they built small paddocks.

Many generations passed until, in 2,200 BC, a wave of new ideas and objects washed into the Time Valley. Axes made of bronze – a harder metal than the copper or tin that had occasionally been used for tools and weapons until then – started to appear in great numbers, brought by traders from Europe who exchanged these and other gifts with the inhabitants of the Time Valley. People who knew how to master the technology involved in making bronze gradually moved into Britain. One year a group of men appeared in the Time Valley and offered to exchange their knowledge – of how to extract copper and tin from certain rocks and combine them at a high temperature to make liquid bronze that could be poured into moulds – for the right to live in the settlement, in terms that suggested they wouldn't take no for an answer. The newcomers spurned the henge as a place of worship and also introduced a new form of burial. They were cremated in huge pyres and buried singly in smaller, round burial mounds – their ashes were placed in huge pottery beakers, many ornately decorated with scratched lines and stamped patterns. In an attempt to prove they had a real right to be in the valley, they claimed that they too were descended from the ancient ancestors in the long barrow on the hilltop, and insisted that their mounds be built as close to them as possible. As time passed the chiefs of these Bronze Age people continued to be interred in round barrows. However, although some were cremated like their predecessors, others were buried with ornate weapons and adornments of bronze and occasionally, as the wealth of the Time Valley people grew on the rich yields of grain, of gold.

The cultivated fields that had simply provided supplementary food and been a safety net in the Neolithic period became more important in the age of axes, knives and arrowheads made from bronze. Trees could be cut down more easily with metal axes, making more land available for cultivation. Yields rose in what was now a warm climate. For the first time the inhabitants of Timechester had a reasonably reliable source of food and the population increased. This meant more mouths to feed – but also provided more people to work the land.

The effort involved in felling trees then ploughing, sowing crops and tending the fields made ownership of the land an increasingly important issue. Long low banks were built to mark where the territory of one settlement began and the next ended. Although it was more than a thousand years since the Neolithic causewayed enclosure had been used for exposing the bodies of those who had died, its previous existence as a place of the dead was dimly remembered in folklore and the site was not used for settlement. In a cursory nod to previous generations its former importance was casually recognized by its reuse as a landmark for laying out one of the boundaries.

The river continued to provide food and was revered because it allowed people from different settlements to travel along it in small round boats and make contact with each other. But as time passed the lake dried up and became marshland which provided a new site for the disposal of the dead. This was a mysterious, treacherous place only penetrable along narrow wooden trackways which had been used and replaced as needed since time immemorial. As the years passed, more and more people who did not want to be buried under mounds came to prefer it as a resting place and their bodies were placed within a wooden structure hidden in the reeds some way from the settlement for this flesh to be eaten away by birds or fish, allowing their spirits to escape. Personal objects, often deliberately broken, accompanied the body as it was carried to the site and were thrown into the water. Over time, more than 300 were dropped into the marsh below the wooden trackway that led to the funeral platform at Timechester. Bronze daggers, in particular, became a popular choice for men, whether or not they had ever used them in anger. Although this was indeed sometimes the case: society was changing, and the seeds of that change had been sown along with the wheat and miniature barley.

barrow excavations

Bronze Age burial mounds are frequently seen in many parts of Britain. They may be made of earth in lowland parts or survive as stony cairns in the uplands and are normally surrounded by a ditch. There is often a hollow depression in the central part of the mound where eighteenth or nineteenth-century archaeologists attempted to locate the main central burial. Although some of these excavations were well intentioned the methods that were used are frowned on today.

Excavations of surviving barrows are rare, as most are now protected by law. However, they are occasionally investigated – when they will be destroyed by road building, for example, or by coastal erosion, as at Sanday in the Orkneys. They are normally excavated by the quadrant method. In this a mound is divided up into four equal parts and two opposing quarters are excavated. The layers in these that show how the mound was constructed are recorded in sections, after which the two remaining quadrants are removed.

Examining an area within a mound may show how the barrow was constructed, perhaps using a circle of timber stakes or with large stones at its core. The barrow may also preserve a section of the landscape it was built on, which will give some indication of the Bronze Age environment and may provide evidence of agriculture, such as plough marks.

Barrows are sometimes almost totally destroyed by modern ploughing and when this has happened the existence of a site can only be established from the air – crops show greater growth if they are above the ditch, where the soil is deeper – or by geophysics. A barrow in this condition can be sampled by a machine-dug trench. It is possible to discover areas of old land surface preserved beneath even the most heavily ploughed mound.

The ditch around a mound usually has steep sides and a flat base and its filling provides valuable evidence about the history of the barrow: it may contain cremation debris, additional burials or be filled with soil from more recent ploughing.

It is important to look beyond the initial burial in the centre of a mound – which may anyway be missing, as it was usually targeted by early excavators. Barrows

A shot of a section through a barrow at Flag Fen

were cemeteries and there are often additional burials and cremations around the edge of the mound and in and beyond the ditch.

At Winterbourne Gunner in Wiltshire *Time Team* found a large Bronze Age urn within an area of barrows, although not directly inside one. Excavating it required skilful digging and lifting by members of a specialist conservation laboratory. First, the edges of the hole containing the find were recorded on a plan and once this had been done the urn was isolated. The soil around it was removed and carefully examined for finds, then the hole was enlarged by digging away some of the natural bedrock. After that the urn was wrapped in bandages and a box was built around it. This was filled with foam which set and allowed the pot to be lifted in one piece. Smaller pots which can be lifted more easily can be wrapped in clingfilm to stabilize them.

The contents of the urn were excavated in a laboratory, in 2 centimetre (almost an inch) spits. Each of these was put through a series of very fine sieves to recover every scrap of bone – with DNA analysis, even the smallest fragments can reveal useful information about the age, sex and health of the person, or people, whose remains they are.

Bronze Age Axe

Socketed axes like this Bronze Age one from Flag Fen in Cambridgeshire were the first to have handles, or hafts, fitted into them. The stem of an axe was hollow and the end of the handle was inserted into this socket to make the tool stronger when the two parts were bound together – axe-heads had rings or loops for cord so that the head could be tied to the haft.

The one shown here was made by the 'lost wax' technique. This involved making a wax model of an axe and wrapping it in clay, which was left to harden and form a mould. This was heated until the wax melted and could be removed leaving just the clay mould. Molten bronze was poured into the mould, filling the cavity left by the wax. Once the bronze had cooled down and hardened, the clay mould was broken and the finished bronze axe was revealed.

Phil on... the Bronze Age

One of my favourite Bronze Age sites – probably one of my all-time favourite sites – is just outside Devizes in Wiltshire. That's probably because I found it and there haven't been many opportunities for me to say that. I was doing some survey work and walked up to the top of a hill then across a piece of ploughed land and there were these enormous bits of Bronze Age pottery just lying around on the surface. Pottery from this period is normally very poorly fired and doesn't survive more than just three or four years' ploughing, so the sheer fact that we were getting big pieces of pot meant that the site had hardly been ploughed at all. We took the pieces of pottery back to the local museum.

At the time, we were looking for a Bronze Age site to excavate as part of a big project to examine settlement on that part of the Marlborough Downs and, if you like, we took a gamble – we didn't know that where we'd found the pottery was a site of occupation, just that something was going on there. We found two beautiful Bronze Age round houses. A round house takes some beating. It isn't very often you get the chance to find a site like that, but to find it and dig it was absolutely cracking! We knew it was Bronze Age because all the pottery was from that period. There were bits of flint work as well. Two rings of post holes were superimposed on top of one another. So the people living on the site must have had one house, then knocked it down and built another one. We had to strip back a big open area to see the relationship between the post holes and mark them on the site plan. Without the pottery to date the site, it could just as easily have been a couple of Iron Age round houses.

I love round houses because they're so sturdy and served this country for thousands of years. It was only when the Romans came along with corners that we ended up with square buildings – and look where that got us! Being able to reconstruct a round house at Beaches Barn on Salisbury Plain was a wonderful experience. I didn't think you could build one that quickly. We put it up in just three days, and it stayed up and was serviceable. I suspect if you wanted something a bit more permanent it would take longer, but we only had the three days. We were scampering around in the roof frame of the structure and some of the bits of wood were quite slender. The whole frame was only tied together and with hindsight the whole thing scares the hell out of me!

People normally associate burial mounds with the Bronze Age and we know quite a lot about burial rites at that time. We're getting to know a lot more about the houses and settlements now but years ago, in the eighteenth and nineteenth centuries, in a landscape littered with Bronze Age barrows, these mounds were the obvious things to investigate. People knew they were burial places and dug them up, so we've got large collections from them. At the same time, probably unwittingly, these excavators did a lot of damage. However, it's still worth digging barrows because they were glorified cemeteries. It's not just one barrow for one body. There can be satellite burials in a mound, and other later burials may have been put into it or sometimes into the ditch – or, as at Winterbourne Gunner in Wiltshire, they might be found just slightly beyond the ditch within the immediate area of the barrow.

wetland archaeology

Fine-grained waterlogged silt and peat are anaerobic deposits, and this lack of oxygen prevents the development of the organisms that cause decay in organic materials like wood and leather. Although these conditions can occur on low-lying sites of any period, some of the most dramatic examples preserve prehistoric trackways which were built to enable people to cross wet, inhospitable marsh land. Sites of this type include Greylake in Somerset and Flag Fen in Cambridgeshire, both of which have been investigated by *Time Team*. They provide a rare insight into aspects of Bronze Age technology and culture which are generally absent elsewhere.

Wetland sites may flood at the level at which the organic remains are preserved and pumps are often used to keep trenches dry. The upper layers of soil, which have been exposed to oxygen and therefore fungal decay, can be removed by a mechanical digger. Once the layers that have been deprived of oxygen are reached, wood will begin to appear. Posts which are well preserved and which have been driven into the marsh can be surprisingly solid and will not break, even when they are touched by a mechanical bucket. However, once they have been reached, hand excavation must begin. At first this can be done with trowels and shovels, but once well-preserved levels are reached some people prefer to use wooden ice-cream sticks to remove the silt or peat without damaging the timbers. Peat is a strange material to excavate. It can be quite dry and is spongy – feeling the ground on the underlying water table move beneath your feet can be a daunting experience.

In some instances the density of the surviving timber means that it becomes impossible to work on the surface of a site. If that happens, specially built frames are installed to allow the diggers to lie suspended above the ground. Once all the finds have been exposed they must be planned and recorded individually before they are lifted. One of the biggest problems faced on excavations like these is identifying which timbers have been placed deliberately and which are driftwood that has become trapped around structural posts. Wetland sites require a comprehensive back-up team to deal with the finds as they are removed from the ground. As soon as

investigating a timber mortuary structure at Greylake, Somerset

organic remains dry out, they shrink, lose colour, crack and fall apart, so they must be kept wet with a spray or placed in tanks of water. Eventually they will be cleaned, drawn, photographed, described and selectively sampled for dendrochronological dating. A small number may be selected for long-term chemical conservation although this is a costly process.

One of the most enjoyable aspects of excavating wetland sites is that after the finds have been cleaned it is possible to study how they were made. Some wooden objects may show that timbers were felled on a regular cycle. Others will show traces of carpentry, wedging and hewing and show the blade marks of stone or metal tools that were used for this – it is sometimes possible to identify the recurring use of individual tools with damaged blades on several timbers. Structural posts and wooden walls, axe handles, arrows and domestic items including bowls, ladles and pins are the kind of objects that have been found on wetland sites and that are lost on dry ones.

It is unfortunate that sites like these are often threatened with destruction as water tables are lowered and peat deposits are excavated for commercial purposes. Some of the most important are now protected by law and are permanently monitored to maintain their state of preservation.

Bronze Age Urns

This urn, which *Time Team* found in a Bronze Age barrow at Winterbourne Gunner in Wiltshire, contained the cremated bones of a Bronze Age person. Cremation was the most common archaeologically visible way of disposing of the dead during this period and, unlike Neolithic pottery which mostly comes from settlements, most Bronze Age pots are found with cremations or inhumations. It is interesting that new styles appear in burials before they come into everyday use in settlements – as if being buried in (or, occasionally, with) the latest pot was more important than showing it off around the house.

Most Bronze Age pottery is fairly coarsely made, with large fragments of stone, shell or grog (broken pottery) included with the clay to prevent it breaking during firing. It is not unlike much Neolithic pottery in appearance, and sometimes the only way to tell the difference between the two is from fragments of rims or bases. The most distinctive Bronze Age pots are beakers, which appear in about 2,400 BC and last until about 1,800 BC. These curve sharply inwards about two-thirds of the way up and then flare out widely at the top. Analyzing the residues inside one beaker placed alongside a Bronze Age burial shows that it had contained mead – perhaps it had been the deceased's favourite drinking vessel, or maybe mead was drunk during the funeral rites – possibly both! Beakers and bronze both appeared in Britain at the same time, but archaeologists are uncertain whether they were brought by immigrants, or were the result of the spread of new ideas.

planning

planning a stone
feature using a
frame at coventry

Making detailed drawings is an important part of the archiving process. Plans of the site are drawn on gridded paper at a ratio of 1:20 – 1 centimetre (⅜ inch) on paper equals 20 centimetres (8 inches) on the ground. To plot walls, pits, post holes and ditches a gridded planning frame is laid over the site – or tapes are used to fix important points – and details are transferred to the paper. Detailed plans of burials can be drawn at a ratio of 1:10. Another site plan at a convenient scale (1:100 or 1:500) shows the position of the grid and locates each trench to permanent buildings and landmarks. The plans are levelled to the ordnance datum to record heights above sea level, which shows the slopes on the site and relates each layer to the next. When a pit, post hole or ditch is excavated, the exposed section is drawn at a scale of 1:10 to show the sequence of layers within it. A horizontal strip is levelled to the ordnance datum and marked with a length of string and measurements are taken above and below this.

Drawings of sections are usually made on waterproof plastic film which can be used in wet conditions and which requires a very hard pencil, usually a 6H or 9H, that will maintain a sharp point.

dendrochronology

Because trees grow by adding a ring of wood around their trunks each year, sometimes only in the spring and summer months, it is possible to count the rings on a tree that has been felled and work out how old it is. Many trees are affected by environmental conditions and their rings reflect how stressed they are: cold, cloudy and very wet years may result in very narrow rings while in really bad years there may be no growth at all.

Dendrochronologists have studied these patterns in various parts of the world and have built up 'master' diagrams that record the different growth rates over many thousands of years. This means that if a well-preserved piece of timber is found, either in a building or an excavation, the pattern of rings can be compared to the master diagrams and the find can be 'dated'. Minute measurements are made and a computer finds the best match for the pattern of rings. If all the sapwood (outermost rings) is present it is usually possible to give the year the tree was felled; if it is missing the date can be estimated from the remaining sapwood; if the sapwood is missing a much rougher date of felling is suggested. In the past, timber was often used while it was still 'green' – unseasoned or not dried out – and as a result the felling date frequently indicates when it was used in the structure that is being dated.

Tree rings clearly visible on this bog oak sample being studied at the dendrochronology laboratory in Belfast

Of potentially greater importance are the oddities found in the ring patterns. Much recent research has concentrated on periods in the last few thousand years when trees were so stressed that hardly any (or even no) growth was put on – the 'narrow ring events'. The conditions necessary to cause this stress include very cold weather or very little sunlight and can be the result of dust veils caused by volcanic eruptions (or possibly even cometary impacts on the earth). Narrow ring events have been dated to 3,195 BC, 2,345 BC, 1,628 BC, 1,159 BC, 207 BC, 44 BC and AD 540. Elaborate arguments have been put forward suggesting that they were the cause of civilizations collapsing, obscurely described historic events, changes of dynasty and so on – all based on the evidence from tree rings!

Mick on... Bronze Age sites

Time Team have dug a number of Bronze Age sites over the years. At one of them, Flag Fen in Cambridgeshire – an incredible site – our excavations uncovered timbers that had formed a trackway across the bogs and pools of the Fens and been preserved in the waterlogged peat for 3,000 years. We also excavated a barrow, which had been used continuously from the Early to the Late Bronze Age. Greylake in Somerset was also waterlogged and here *Time Team* found a line marked by timbers, which might have related to an early territorial boundary. Other timbers seemed to relate to a platform of some kind, and when we found human bones the site became very intriguing. It was probably where the dead were thrown into the bog as part of a burial ritual. This practice is seen increasingly on Bronze Age sites – platforms have also been found in the bogs at Flag Fen and it is likely that they too were used for other ceremonies and rituals connected with life, birth, coming of age and other significant events.

The Bronze Age is the first period during which there is clear evidence of man's interaction with the landscape. Apart from monuments built in the Neolithic and the Early Bronze Age, like long barrows and henges which have survived as field monuments and are part of the actual infrastructure of the Bronze Age landscape, alignments and boundaries like the ones *Time Team* found at Greylake are probably the earliest existing signs of settlement. A wandering country lane or parish boundary could date back to the Bronze Age. The Dartmoor reeves (field boundary banks) are the best examples of this in Britain as it is known that they go back to that period. The ones around the edge of Dartmoor run straight down into fields that are in current use and which are basically Bronze Age fields that have survived to the modern day.

Features like these were probably a result of a growing population and increasing pressure on the land that was available: when a certain density of population and a certain intensity of farming activity are reached it becomes necessary to define ownership by visibly marking out the division of land. This is fundamentally the theme of the Late Bronze Age, which was also the period when the first hillforts were built and a great range of weaponry was developed. It's difficult to escape the conclusion that not only was there pressure on the resources that were available in some parts of Britain in the Bronze Age, but that people were also prepared to fight for, and defend, these resources.

The bronze axe that *Time Team* reconstructed as the cameo in the Flag Fen programme in 1999 was an example of the kind of weapons that were produced by skilled craftsmen during this period. I was amazed at how small the furnace we used to melt the bronze was, and the amount of heat it could generate. The bronze axe that finally appeared was a beautiful object and gave me some idea of the status metalsmiths must have enjoyed during the Bronze Age.

CHAPTER 4
iron age

carenza's story of Timechester in the year 0

After another 1,500 years, the landscape of the Time Valley has again changed profoundly, although many elements are still recognizable from previous periods. The earliest monument of all, the Neolithic long barrow, still stands proud on the horizon surrounded by numerous smaller Bronze Age burial mounds. The low ditches of the causewayed enclosure are also just visible on the adjacent hilltop. But none of the buildings from the Bronze Age settlement are still in existence, and the slight holes from the posts that once held them up have long since been lost from sight. The settlement has not moved far; it has just shifted slightly and grown to about twenty round houses of varying size. However, it is now surrounded by a ditch and additionally protected by a palisade fence. A new settlement, in the shape of a banjo and defined by massive ditches and a timber fence, occupies a low knoll on the far side of the river which flows through hillsides that are almost completely covered by a carefully regulated dense patchwork of fields; there is hardly any woodland left. Although the boundaries between the different settlement territories are still where they were before, they are larger and much more difficult to cross. The biggest change is on the hilltop: two huge circuits of ditch and bank enclose the land occupied by the long barrow and its satellite round barrows and it is this that dominates the skyline. The area inside these ramparts is tightly packed with thatched round houses. What is the story behind these profound changes which nonetheless owe so much to earlier generations?

In the years after 1,500 BC the changing traditions that had led to the use of open funerary platforms in marshland soon gained hold, and burial in the ground ceased to be acceptable. The dead of Timechester were instead taken to secluded places away from settlements and exposed to the elements and scavengers. This released their spirits and their physical remains became invisible to succeeding generations. But although the dead left no enduring mark on the landscape, the

 fields they tended in life and the settlements in which they lived became more and more strongly established as successive years of ploughing caused banks to build up along the edges of fields and ditches were dug around clusters of houses for drainage and demarcation. Not all the fields were cultivated every year. The people realized that doing this would reduce yields and failing fields were rested for a few years, to be grazed and manured by the sheep and cattle that the inhabitants of Timechester

now owned in large numbers. This was effective, but in about 900 BC the warm climate that had prevailed for a millennium or more came to an end, ushering in a period of colder, wetter weather. Now it was up to human ingenuity to sustain the agricultural revolution that had started under significantly more auspicious conditions, and on which the Time Valley's inhabitants now depended so heavily. The people of Timechester turned to new crops, bartering with traders for spelt wheat instead of Emmer, and for the seed beans which were then being cultivated

for the first time. And at about this time the traders brought word of an idea that was new to the Time Valley but had long been established in parts of Europe: using

animals to pull ploughs. It seemed an unlikely solution to the poorer weather, but cows proved strong and fairly tractable once they had been trained, and were much faster at ploughing than humans: lower yields could be compensated for by cultivating larger areas.

With increasing speed, woodland and scrub were cleared and the land tamed. The small square fields of the Bronze Age were reorganized into large rectangular fields laid out, almost regardless of changes in terrain, in huge gridded blocks. The warmer, south-facing slopes of the valley were the most productive but as time passed even steep north-facing hillsides were brought into cultivation. Sustained by a regular supply of food, the population rose. Unnoticeably at first, pressure on the land grew as the amount of uncultivated land that was available for clearance began to shrink. Eventually it dwindled to almost nothing as nearly the whole valley fell to the plough.

In about 800 BC a new kind of metal technology became available in the Time Valley for the first time. Iron was harder than bronze and tools made from it were stronger, with sharper cutting edges that did not blunt so quickly. Obtaining such an essential but limited resource was beyond the scope of simple gift exchange: those with access to iron ores knew what their value was and drove a hard bargain. The inhabitants of the valley were lucky: despite the poorer climate the large field systems could still produce surpluses of wheat, barley, oats and beans for trade, and the sheep that thrived on the hillside pastures provided wool which could be made into clothes that could be traded for metal axes, knives and spears. In the rapidly growing village at Timechester few of the round thatched houses lacked a loom, which was worked by anyone unfit for work in the fields. Bone awls, the other essential tool for making garments, were much more easy to lose. They were used to pierce pieces of leather so that they could be sewn together with thongs to make shoes and, sometimes, outer clothing.

The precious grain on which everyone was increasingly dependent was stored in pits dug into the ground or in raised granaries. Meat was provided by herds of sheep and cattle and by smaller numbers of pigs, which were good at turning domestic rubbish into good meat but had no other product such as wool or milk. The intensively farmed land left little scope for hunting or foraging, but the river and adjacent marsh continued to provide a steady supply of fish and wild birds. The challenge of poorer weather had been met with great success, and settlements up and down the Time Valley grew in size.

To thank the gods for their generosity, religious rituals were performed. These were closely tied in with everyday activities: most people made sure they gave an offering such as a new quern stone or a favourite dog to their storage pit when it came to the end of its life, in thanks for the grain it had kept fresh for so long and to ensure good harvests to keep the new pit full of grain. No one felt the need to create special places solely for worship.

Such success was not without its penalties, and as land became more valuable people's insecurity grew. In about 700 BC some of the inhabitants of Timechester dug a ditch around their settlement and protected it further with a strong wattle fence. However, as the settlement continued to expand, this boundary fell out of use and in about 400 BC it was replaced by a larger outer enclosure.

By then Timechester was not the only enclosed site in the Time Valley. In about 500 BC, insecurity combined with a desire to show off his strength led one chief to build a new kind of settlement. He forced vast numbers of his people to dig a huge ditch, piling up the excavated stone into an inner bank, around almost the whole circumference of the most prominent point in the landscape: the hilltop which had for so long been occupied by the long barrow and its satellite round barrows. The chief of this, Timebury, hillfort claimed it would be of benefit to the entire clan. Grain could be stored there and cattle brought in for protection during occasional raids by neighbouring chiefs. But most people were aware that the main purpose of the fort was to glorify their leader and show the heads of other clans how powerful he was. Worse still, constant backbreaking work was needed to keep the banks clear of grass and allow the glowing white bedrock to stand out against the green of the surrounding landscape.

Some 150 years later, the people of the Time Valley had forgotten the cold, wet weather of the early Iron Age as the climate improved from after about 400 BC. Population levels began to rise but, fuelled by the rising crop yields the warmer weather allowed, inequalities in the expanding society became more marked. Chiefs

An aerial view of sidbury Hillfort on salisbury plain

became more powerful and increasingly prepared to defend their possessions by fighting. Although organized raiding was still rare, it was hardly unknown. Two smaller hillforts in neighbouring valleys were abandoned after they were sacked by a particularly rapacious Timebury chief. The defeated occupants were taken prisoner and worked to death building a second bank-and-ditch circuit around his hillfort and an ornate maze-like entrance, all made of huge earthen banks. At the same time, the boundaries between hilltop Timebury and valley-bottom Timechester were aggressively reinforced by the construction of huge ditches and banks along the lines of the old Bronze Age boundaries.

By 100 BC the population was still rising and by then inhabitants of the valley had no memory of a time before the hillfort. Once again, however, things changed. New ideas from Europe began to sweep across the valley as efficient seagoing plank-built boats superseded earlier hide-covered craft and made contact and trade easier. Strange coins appeared, similar to those in continental Europe. They were made out of gold which, unlike iron, had no real value as it could not be used for making tools, but the coins were valued for their own sake, as status symbols. The headman of the Timechester settlement had only a few, but the chief of Timebury was reputed to have handfuls of them, obtained by trading corn, hunting dogs, cattle and, most of all, slaves captured in raids...

This contact with Europe also gave the people of the Time Valley new ways of propitiating the gods. The simple ritual of placing offerings in storage pits no longer seemed adequate and in about 80 BC an unpopular, brutal chief, Prasudubnus, keen to at least keep the gods on his side, built a small square shrine inside Timebury hillfort. It was just a couple of metres square with a porch on the east side, but secret rituals, of which only the chief and the shaman knew the secrets, were carried out inside this small space. In years when there were particularly good harvests a cow was sacrificed outside the shrine and buried near the porch.

However, shortly after the shrine was finished, Prasudubnus himself moved out of the hillfort which had been occupied by his predecessors for more than twenty generations. Although a few of his followers stayed on there, he felt that such a windswept and open settlement occupied by thirty extended families was no longer appropriate for a leader who needed to show off his status by displaying his appreciation of the finer, continental things in life. More and more he was enjoying wine and other goods traded from Europe, and he liked to believe that he was respected by the Romans who occupied so much of that continent. A new elite residence, just for his immediate family, was needed, built on a more civilized spot at Upchester, which was nearer the river and in the lee of Timebury hill. And he knew what the new style should be. A large round house was built with several huge storage pits and a couple of working and storage huts, all within an enclosure that was far smaller than the hillfort. This private enclosure was shaped like a banjo and defined by a huge ditch, almost sheer-sided and nearly 3 metres (10 feet) deep. Most importantly, it was entered via a long 'bottleneck' entrance pathway that was covered with flint cobbles and flanked on either side by huge ditches. Prasudubnus was sure that with such a residence his position would be unassailable, but at the back of his mind he reckoned that if the Romans did become aggressive he could always retreat to the hillfort.

Both Prasudubnus and the chief of Timechester had indeed been worried when Julius Caesar, after an unsuccessful attempt to invade Britain in 55 BC, had been successful in 54 BC. After a few disastrous battles with the Romans they and other British chiefs had agreed to pay tribute to Rome and the Roman legions had gone back to the continent. Although they had bragged to their followers that this was a great military victory, they were aware that the Romans had achieved most of their aims. This was galling, but the tributewas not an especially heavy burden for the Time Valley, where grain yields were still high.

In fact, the increased contact with Rome seemed to have its advantages. Prasudubnus, now living in his banjo enclosure, and the headman at Timechester became increasingly closely allied with the Romans, adopting much of their way of life and importing more and more of their luxury goods. Their wives wore brooches with ornate curved continental decorations, and large red clay vessels (amphorae) full of wine were a common sight. For the chiefs, the perfect solution seemed to have been worked out.

Phil on... the Iron Age

The Iron Age is a period I greatly look forward to because there is always a chance of a nice juicy storage pit. There's nothing better if you get a good 'un. They're 2 to 3 metres (6½ to 10 feet) deep and often bell-shaped. There's so much stuff in them, gorgeous big lumps of pot and bone – particularly pot, which is all handmade stuff – that if you trowelled the pieces out it would take an eternity. However, you can dig them fairly meticulously with a pick and shovel. You may not get each and every individual bucketful that's represented in the fill, but you'll get the general sequence. You can be pretty efficient, and get all the information at the same time.

Having said that, not all storage pits have loads and loads of swag in them. I've done some in the past that have been a total embarrassment to dig. Finding a good one is, of course, dependent on the geology. On a nice piece of chalk you'll get classic archaeology – sort of beginner's level – a big ol' pit, filled up with big stuff and surrounded by white chalk. However, if you're in an area where the soil's not right for corn you ain't gonna get one.

Another thing you sometimes get in Iron Age pits is bodies. But you obviously can't predict whether you're going to get one. So there you are, busily going down in what you believe to be an Iron Age storage pit and, lo and behold, you suddenly start hitting human bones. Although you treat them like you would ones from any other human burial, exactly how they are laid in the pit is often unpredictable. In some cases they appear to just be bundled in. So it takes a little longer to work out which bit of the skeleton you've found and, from that point on, where the rest of it is and how it's lying in the pit.

A lot of Iron Age people were in fact buried in storage pits. Certainly, on chalk it's not unusual to find a body in one. That's not to say that everyone was buried in pits, because I'm sure they weren't, but they do occur there. The bodies seem to have been fairly unceremoniously dumped in, without a formal extended burial.

Years ago everybody dug the ramparts – the defences – on a hillfort but nowadays people are a lot more aware of what was going on inside it, who was living there, what they were doing there, what the layout of the place was. So more recently much of our knowledge about the Iron Age has come from excavating inside hillforts rather than just digging the defences.

Round houses, storage pits, four-post structures (little squares of four posts which are normally regarded as being granaries) – in some instances the structures are laid out in quite a formalized way. I reckon hillforts were undoubtedly defensive settlements, as in some cases there were a lot of people living there – obviously enough for the Romans to think it worthwhile attacking them. On the other hand, sometimes you find a hillfort that seems to have had virtually no people living in it at all.

At Waddon in Dorset, *TIme Team* found a lovely Iron Age floor surface. Any floor surface is a nice find, no matter where it is, because this is where people walked about, and dropped things and made things, and made a big mess and all the rest of it. Unfortunately you don't get one very often – it's wonderful when you do.

iron age ditches

Although agriculture was established in the Neolithic period it is not until the Bronze Age that the layout of field systems and land boundaries becomes more apparent. And by the Iron Age and Roman periods complete field systems, land boundaries and settlements were found throughout Britain. Some of the most important of these can be plotted by earthwork survey when the banks and ditches are visible as 'lumps and bumps'; or by studying aerial photographs when the features have been ploughed away by more recent agriculture. These techniques allow archaeologists to relate field systems to settlements and show where land boundaries were realigned through time as farm ownership changed. *TIme Team* identified such a change at Lavenham in Suffolk.

These ancient field systems, land boundaries and settlements are often defined by ditches. It is usual to excavate where these intersect as this shows whether one is older than the other. Sometimes individual ditches were allowed to fill up and have subsequently been redug along the same alignment. This shows that boundaries have stayed in the same place for many years. Ditches are excavated in layers using picks and shovels. There is usually coarse material at the base which represents natural bedrock that has fallen in from the sides of the freshly cut ditch. As the primary fill (soil from the walls of the ditch fallen in through lack of use) stabilized, the process of infilling slowed down and the upper fills are composed of much finer-grained material. If the ditch is near to a settlement, large amounts of datable rubbish may have been thrown into it. (This applies even in the twentieth century: at Wierre-Effroy in northern France, *Time Team* recovered large pieces of a Spitfire that had been thrown into a ditch by a farmer.) In more outlying areas finds may be scarce and large amounts of plough soil may have worked their way into the ditch.

If there is pottery in the primary fill the date at which the ditch went out of

carenza excavating the drip gully of a round house at kemerton

Bone Artefacts

Bone is resilient but flexible and, because of its great strength, can be worked easily to produce durable, hardwearing objects. Bones from wild animals were used to make tools as long as 450,000 years ago; and from the time that sheep, cows and goats were first domesticated theirs were made into a variety of implements.

The bone awl was found at Waddon in Dorset, in the middle of an Iron Age round house. It would have been suitable for all kinds of activities but its main use was probably in making clothes from hides or leather. Its point, which has worn to a smooth shiny surface over time, was sharp enough to pierce holes through which thongs could be threaded; the awl could also be used to attach bone or antler toggles to clothes.

The bone comb was found in the ditch of a banjo enclosure at Beaches Barn on Salisbury Plain, Wiltshire. With its distinctive long handle, it was not designed for combing hair (although it could have been used for this), but was for use during weaving to batter down the horizontal wef, or woof, threads between the vertical warp threads. This kept the woven cloth strong and increased its durability. Interestingly, whoever made this comb decorated it with incised lines and ring-and-dot patterns. The extra effort this would have involved suggests that it was a valued possession, and it is strange that it found its way into the ditch while it was still in fairly good condition – maybe it was a ritual offering.

use is usually calculated by this. Any from higher up provides a rough guide but may be misleading if the ditch is filled with plough soil, which usually contains a range of materials from different dates. Pottery which has been reworked in this soil for many years is likely to be small with well-rounded edges, and will be of limited value for dating.

Ditches were dug for a variety of reasons including defence, ceremony, enclosure of stock and to depict property boundaries. Evidence for their precise function may be found beyond their edges. It is likely that soil from the construction of the ditch was mounded up to form a bank on one or both sides and traces of this bank may be present in the excavation. There may have been a fence or palisade which may survive in a row of post holes. Soil samples from a ditch may contain valuable environmental evidence to show that there were overhanging hedges and trees or that it lay in open country.

recording

filling in context
sheets, one of the most
important tasks on
an excavation

One of the most important aspects of an excavation is the process of recording on paper all that is revealed and destroyed during the dig. The result is an archive that allows anyone in the future to re-examine every detail of each layer as it was seen and dug, and to know what the archaeologists thought they meant at the time. This means that the results of an excavation can be reinterpreted in the future from the original records.

The archive comprises a written description of all pits, ditches, walls and post holes and the layers that fill them (sequence contexts). A post hole, for example, involves the construction of the hole, the placing of the post in the hole and putting the packing around the post. These three events are recorded as a sequence and can be related to the overall sequence of layers and other features on the site. Each context/layer is located within the site using coordinates from a grid and its extent, thickness, texture, colour and relationship to the surrounding layers is described. This means that it is necessary to record whether a layer overlies (is later than), underlies (is earlier than), cuts through (is later than) or is cut by (is earlier than) another layer. In this way each layer can be related to another and each can be dated by the finds they contain. This allows the story of the site to be reconstructed. It is important to use the youngest, most recent finds to date a layer as older ones are likely to have been redeposited.

On really complicated sites the layers can be plotted on a matrix, which is like a family tree. It shows each layer of similar date from different parts of the site on a horizontal axis, and indicates how it is related to earlier layers, which are plotted below, and later layers, which are shown above.

In addition, a complete photographic record – both colour slides and black-and-white prints – is made of the excavation.

A preprinted form is now generally used to record each context/layer. The form for each context/layer is given a unique number which allows context/layers to be cross-referenced to the drawings, photographs and finds, ensuring that a comprehensive excavation archive is produced.

Quern Stones

The earliest means of grinding cereal to make flour for bread involved rubbing the grains between two stones. In its most primitive form, the saddle quern, a hand-held stone dating from the early Iron Age, was rubbed backwards and forwards across the grain on the larger stone or 'quern'. A smooth even hollow developed in the lower stone and the 'rubber' became highly polished.

A more sophisticated rotary quern, like the one below from Beaches Barn, was introduced in the later Iron Age period whereby one circular stone was rotated on top of another. This one is in perfect

condition and seems to have been a ritual offering. Grains were fed through a central pivot hole and emerged at the circumference of the bottom stone as flour. A backwards–forwards motion using a wooden handle inserted into the side of the top stone seems to have been the preferred motion.

Hand mills using quern stones persisted into the Middle Ages, even though water-powered mills with larger millstones were introduced during the Roman period and wind power (from windmills) came into use in the twelfth century.

aerial archaeology

Aerial photography is the single most cost-effective way of identifying new sites (thousands are found every year), and also provides an extremely useful way of analyzing them. Photographs that are taken looking straight down give the truest image of the ground and the information can easily be transferred to a map. The first systematic vertical air-survey of this country was carried out just after the Second World War, and provides a fascinating record of Britain in 1946–7. Nowadays most counties are photographed vertically in their entirety every ten years from a set height, which produces photographs at a standard mapping scale: most Ordnance Survey maps, including road maps, rely heavily on aerial information. However, accurate vertical photography requires special equipment, so archaeological air photographers usually take oblique shots that are as close to the vertical as possible, and correct the images by referring archaeological details on the sites to mapped features such as field boundaries, houses or roads.

Earthwork sites show up well from the air, particularly in low sunlight, which often provides the best chance to get a good overall image. But aerial archaeology's greatest contribution is without doubt its ability to see and record sites that are invisible or incomprehensible from the ground. These are ones which have been ploughed flat but whose remains can be seen as marks in pasture and in growing or ripening crops.

The reason sites like these show up from the air is because of the effect a buried ditch or wall has on the growth of vegetation. A ditch is likely to be full of soil that is richer and more moist than the undisturbed ground surface: plants or crops (or grass) growing over this will be taller and more lush than anything that surrounds them, and ripen more slowly. Conversely, if there is a thinner depth of soil over a buried wall this soil dries out more quickly than above in the rest of the field. Plants and crops growing over walls – or banks – have less soil from which to get nourishment, and less water, and so are thinner and shorter-stemmed than other plants. They also ripen more quickly. In very dry years plants growing on a buried ditch have an even greater advantage over those that are over a wall or bank and show up particularly well as crop marks on plough-levelled sites. The same principle applies to grass; at Turkdean in Gloucestershire, for example, the vital clue to the presence of an otherwise unknown villa was the way grass died off in a dry summer where it overlaid the Roman walls.

Because the differentiation that produces crop marks is so dependent on the weather, sites that are well defined one year can be completely invisible the next. In addition, the marks may be visible for only a week or less because the wall or bank crops ripen just a few days ahead of the ditch ones. At Kemerton in Worcestershire a massive complex of hundreds of years' worth of Bronze Age and Iron Age settlement, including numerous enclosures, round houses, paddocks and storage pits, showed up clearly on air photographs that were taken one summer. However, when *Time Team* went to investigate the site some years later wetter conditions meant that absolutely no marks were visible. The type of crop also makes a difference – wheat and barley are good at producing crop marks, while leafy vegetables (like the turnips at Kemerton) tend to be poor.

Aerial view of Winterbourne Gunner site with the ring ditch of a Bronze Age barrow showing in the adjacent field.

excavating post holes

I f a site is waterlogged, timbers will be well preserved, making it relatively easy to see how wooden buildings were constructed. On a dry site the wood will have rotted away, and the only evidence for the building will be the post holes that were dug to hold the timbers upright.

The first problem when excavating dryland post holes is actually identifying them in the trench. Typically, they are found when the topsoil has been removed and the top of the archaeological layer is being trowelled clean. Small patches that look different, feel harder or softer, or are stonier than the surrounding ground may be noticeable. If they are roughly round or oval, and anything between 20 centimetres (8 inches) and 2 metres (6½ feet) across they might be post holes. Their positions should be recorded on the site plan and this could show that several of these possible post holes are in a line. That's when you start to think you might have a building.

Half-sectioned post-hole from a grubenhaus at Kemerton

The next stage is to excavate the post holes. Unless they are very small, the best way to do this is by 'half-sectioning' them. A string is put across the middle of a patch and the fill on only one side of it is removed – it is usually reasonably easy to feel the edge of the hole. A drawing is then made of the shape of the vertical face, or section, across the middle of the post hole, which becomes visible when the fill has been been removed from one side. This is the only way to show the depth and shape of the hole and might show the 'post-pipe' where the post has rotted away. Any packing stones or finds are drawn on the plan from above, and marked on the section drawing. After the section has been drawn, the rest of the post hole can be excavated.

Any finds from the fill are important because they probably got there either when the hole was being dug and the posts were wedged in (in this case they will nestle at the bottom and among packing stones) or soon after the post had rotted away and the hole was filling up with surface detritus – finds above the packing stones or near the top of the hole indicate that this is probable. The height and position of everything in the post hole must therefore be recorded accurately. It is possible that the finds can date both the beginning and the end of the life of a timber building. It is also possible that an object from a much earlier period has got into the post hole – you can never take anything for granted in archaeology.

When the hole is empty it should be obvious whether the post it held stood upright or at an angle. Once all the post holes that can be seen in a trench have been excavated, the archaeologist can try to visualize the building by working out how many posts there were and which way they leant. It can be a bit like dot-to-dot – two parallel lines of four post holes could mean a long rectangular building, or two smaller square ones. Deciding which type it was often depends on knowing what the different kinds of timber buildings looked like.

Mick on... Iron Age sites

Time Team hasn't excavated many Iron Age sites, although there was a good one at Waddon in Dorset where neighbours found Iron Age and medieval pottery in their gardens and asked us to investigate. We uncovered an Iron Age round house and, even better, it was possible to see how it had been successively rebuilt as occupation on the site continued throughout the period. Another Iron Age site *Time Team* visited was Boleigh in Cornwall, where we excavated a fogou – an underground tunnel constructed for an unknown purpose. I wanted to understand the landscape around this enigmatic feature better. Where had the people who built it lived? Would there be any evidence around the entrance to the fogou that could give a clue to its function? After three days we had located the settlement and lots of pottery and building material. Stewart Ainsworth had also managed to trace the course of the fogou, while geophysics had revealed another one at a nearby site – it had already been found in the nineteenth century, but its location had been forgotten.

The excavation on Salisbury Plain in Wiltshire, when *Time Team* helped the army to investigate a field in the training area for tanks, was a real treat. Three days of digging revealed two banjo enclosures – aristocratic Iron Age settlements – and lots of pottery from the period.

Finding just one of these enclosures would have been great – finding two was very exciting.

In general, the Iron Age saw some major changes in the landscape, which started in about 900 BC when the climate became colder and wetter. People were forced to abandon settlements in marginal areas like Dartmoor and other highland regions – there are very few Iron Age remains in places like these – because it was impossible to grow the crops they had come to depend on, and the population throughout the country collapsed.

Wooded areas were cleared to make more land available for agriculture. As the Iron Age population gradually grew, the pressure on land increased. This prompted tribes to protect their territories and settlements with fortifications such as fences or ditches as a defence against aggressive neighbours. However, there were no ceremonial burial monuments like the barrows and henges of the early prehistoric period. So, although Iron Age settlements, hillforts and field systems can be seen in the modern landscape, there are no ritual monuments. Conversely, while the ceremonial, burial and ritual monuments of early prehistoric people are visible, their settlements can't be seen clearly.

Unlike in the Bronze Age, when people were buried under barrows, there are no clearly defined Iron Age cemeteries – there are only occasional cremated burials, and burials in ditches and pits. Skeletons and a variety of bones can be found all over an Iron Age site. Because of this it would be easy to assume that Iron Age men and women didn't care about the dead. I don't agree: just because only a part of somebody is buried doesn't mean that this wasn't done with as much reverence and concern as if they had been placed under a barrow.

roman

carenza's story of Timechester in 350

Just 350 years have passed since our last look at Timechester, but in that short time it has changed almost out of recognition: only in the countryside are traces of the past clearly visible. In place of the busy but untidy Late Iron Age settlement there is a huge, geometrically planned town with a thriving open marketplace. It is seething with the people, some of them immensely wealthy, who live and work in its closely packed stone-built houses. The rectangular street plan of gridded blocks of buildings is surrounded by high walls and arranged along a single cardinal feature – a ramrod-straight road that cuts out of the town and sweeps across the landscape. On the other side of the river, part of the grassed-over banks of the banjo enclosure are just visible under the walls of a large stone villa with ornate gardens. The Iron Age hillfort is still occupied, but a Roman temple dominates the small houses within it. The only parts of the valley that seems really unchanged are the fields which are still as regularly laid out as they were in the later Iron Age. Only those on the newly drained marshland are new and different – long thin rectangular enclosures defined by small hedges. How has the Time Valley changed so much in such a relatively short time?.

The Iron Age seems to have ended abruptly in the valley soon after 43 AD when the Roman emperor Claudius, driven by a need for military victories and an impatience with renewed British support for rebel Gaulish chiefs, invaded Britain. This time paying the Romans to go away was out of the question. The new chief at Upchester, who was less enthusiastic about the Romans than his grandfather Prasudubnus had been and who had been actively helping rebels in Gaul, retreated from his Upchester banjo enclosure to the Timebury hillfort. But although his followers fought ferociously and despite the massive defending banks and ditches, the fort was soon stormed and sacked by the Roman legionaries. Its gateway was burned down and any defenders left alive were taken as slaves while the dead where left where they had fallen.

The headman at Timechester, a wily fellow named Cogitagus, realized where his best interests lay. He quickly agreed to the Roman suggestion that if he and the inhabitants of the Time Valley submitted to their control he could continue as leader, and moved his family into the vacated Upchester banjo site. Nonetheless the Romans made sure that any unrest that might break out could be quickly quelled by building a large military fort called Tempuscaster (the Latin for Timechester) to accommodate a legion of soldiers. It had long straight walls with curving corners like those on playing cards, and was soon linked to other similar sites in Britain by a wide road, well built with several layers of hard-rammed stone surfaces. Ignoring the earlier trackways that wound along hilltops and river valleys or dog-legged around fields, the road ran dead straight out of the north and south gates of the fort, cutting straight across anything and everything in its path. While Cogitagus fumed with impotent rage,

fields were obliterated or cut in half and even natural obstacles such as rivers and hills rarely forced it to deviate from its course. With communications like this, the Roman legions could move rapidly across the country to put down any resistance.

But the legionaries were soon moved permanently away from the largely peaceful and acquiescent Time Valley, into Wales where Iron Age tribes and priests continued to resist the Roman takeover. However, even in this short time the settlement at Timechester had adapted to the presence of the fort, selling food to the soldiers and providing inns and other places where they could relax when they were off duty.

Although Cogitagus had coveted the Upchester banjo enclosure for many years and moved into it as soon as it was vacated, a generation later his son became discontented with it. Surely his status within a Roman province demanded a Roman-style home? Within a few years Cogitagus's son had built a large timber villa at Upchester with a suite of rectangular rooms close to the enclosure – the silting-up banjo ditches were used as a rubbish dump. Here visitors, many of whom were, like himself, adminstrators in the newly taken-over province, could be treated to meals served on glossy red Samian pottery from Gaul and wine imported from Italy and Spain. All this could be paid for by profits from grain grown on the large estate which surrounded his villa – the same land which had supported the chief of Timebury.

The roman road at preston st mary

Cogitagus's son also turned his attention to the settlement around the Roman fort at Timechester and began the long process of converting it into a town worthy of the valley's new status as a Roman province. It was not a task he would live to see completed, but over decades the gridded street plan was laid out with help from Roman-trained surveyors, and engineers installed piped water supplies and constructed formal buildings including an open colonnaded marketplace or forum, baths and a temple. In paying for such edifices Cogitagus's son, now officially known as a client king or *princeps civitas*, and others of his status – some British-born like him, some newly arrived administrators from Europe – showed off their cultured superiority by adopting the Roman lifestyle, which they promoted as being much more civilized than that of the Iron Age. They also worshipped Roman gods who, they assured themselves, seemed very like the old Iron Age ones. Rumours of persecuted bands of fanatical religious zealots called Christians occasionally reached

Timechester, but following this religion could be dangerous: in about 200 AD a Christian called Albanus had been killed for refusing to worship the emperor as a god – the spot where he fell was not forgotten and was secretly revered by other Christians. The Timechester dead were generally buried according to Roman custom, in the cemetery just outside the newly built walls of the new town. Inside the walls, workshops soon sprang up for the craftsmen who sold their products in the forum, and taxes on what was sold in the market began to generate large sums of money which, in their turn, paid for more buildings.

The fields continued to be cultivated as before. They had to be – it was the profits from the grain that paid for the town of Timechester to be built and for the heavy taxes that had to go to Rome. In about 143, in an effort to increase the amount of available land, work began on draining the marshland that had for so long been a sanctuary for birds and for the bones of the long-forgotten dead of the later Bronze Age and the Iron Age. Before the end of the second century AD, this newly turned rich, dark, fertile soil was producing astronomic yields of grains, richly rewarding those who had invested in the building of drains and canals. Behind the villa some of the south-facing hill slopes were terraced and planted with vines which, tended properly, rarely failed to produce a good crop in the warm climate.

By this time more and more people were living in Timechester, rather than just working and trading there, and from about 200 AD wealthy citizens began building huge ornate town houses with mosaic floors, glass windows and painted walls. The new town seethed with life. Slaves hurried to and fro and people came there to buy or sell in the market, visit the temple, spend a day in the baths or carry out the business of running the administrative region of Timechester and its hinterland, the Timechester civitas.

New buildings were also being constructed in the surrounding countryside. Soon after 250, Cogitagus's descendents at the Upchester timber villa had acquired enough money to begin building a residence they considered to be a proper reflection of their status as magistrates of Timechester and owners of a large estate which occupied most of the valley either side of the River Time at Timechester. Accordingly, they built a vast stone villa around a colonnaded courtyard, with elaborate gardens and pools, suites of centrally heated rooms and a separate bath house with hot and cold plunge baths. But within a couple of

Birdoswald on Hadrian's wall from the air

generations their grandchildren thought that even this was inadequate as money from the intensively farmed estate continued to pour in. Seventy years later another courtyard was added, doubling the size of the villa and enabling the service quarters, such as kitchens and stables, to be kept well away from the luxurious rooms in which the Cogitagus's descendents lived and entertained. Here rich food was eaten by the richly dressed and bejewelled owners and their guests, while games were played with dice, boards and beautiful glass counters.

However, by no means everyone lived in such style. The Roman invasion had brought great wealth to some, but for the majority of the inhabitants of the valley the standard of living changed little and slowly. Most were tied farm labourers who worked on the vast villa estate, lived in the same place, farmed the same land and used the same trackways their ancestors had used for generations. Some lived in farmsteads, others in purpose-built estate villages. However, even for them, new styles of hard-fired wheel-thrown pottery were available cheaply at the market, paid for with coins rather than by bartering as had been the way before. Some of these were so maddeningly tiny that they were handed over by the bagful, and only children bothered to scrabble for dropped ones. People who could find the resources rebuilt their houses in the new rectangular style when the old circular ones came to the end of their lives; many others had to continue to patch up round houses.

Up at Timebury hillfort, which had been reoccupied a few years after the conquest, things had actually got worse: stories were still told of the time when people living in Timebury had the highest standard of living in the valley, but the settlement was now a poor shadow of life in the villa or in Timechester. No running water, no paved streets – just huts, mud and the cold wind. The only stone structure in the hillfort was a temple. It had been built immediately after the conquest on the site of the Iron Age shrine, in the Roman style, and was dedicated to one of the Roman gods. Although the people had been told that he was the same as one of the British deities, they knew the temple was really there to remind them that the Romans were now in charge and likely to stamp hard on any attempt at revolt. But in the intensively farmed, densely occupied landscape, where all the land was owned by someone, there was nowhere else to go.

By 350 Timechester had been part of the Roman Empire for so long that no one could remember a time before towns and villas, stone buildings and paved streets, roads and, of course, taxes. The emperor, Constantine the Great, had converted to Christianity in 313 after defeating a rival claimant to his title of emperor, and ruled that the formerly obscure religion should be tolerated throughout the empire. By the middle of the century no self-respecting town would be without a church, and the leaders of Timechester were determined to maintain the city's pride: work began on a Christian church, built on the still-remembered spot where Albanus had died so many years ago. It had to face due east, which meant it did not fit perfectly into the gridded street plan. The people of Timechester hoped that the new god would protect the town from the political unrest and raids by pirates and tribes from northern Europe which were becoming so much more common.

Roman Pottery

Roman pottery is distinctively different to any other, not only because of its quality but also because it is so widespread: it flooded into Britain in the years after the conquest of AD 43 and was soon ubiquitous. Roman artefacts that pre-date the invasion have also been found on some sites, but only in small quantities.

Unlike prehistoric pottery, Roman wares were hard-fired in kilns (rather than in bonfires), and were made and finished on a wheel rather than by hand, so they are harder than earlier examples, and generally finer – the walls are thinner and there are few, if any, bits of grit or shell in the clay. Samian ware, the best-known type, is an expensive tableware which was imported from France throughout the first and second centuries AD. It is a deep salmon-red and is coated with a layer of liquid clay or slip that gives it a shiny appearance. The pottery is sometimes decorated with patterns or scenes that include figures: the cavorting humans on the piece from Birdoswald on Hadrian's wall, and the hunting scene on the fragment from Papcastle, Cumbria, which *Time Team* reconstructed, are examples. Samian ware went out of use at the beginning of the third century. It had been popular until then and the reason why it vanished more or less overnight is not known. It may well have been that trade was disrupted when Albinus, the Roman governor of Britain, attempted to take over from Severus, the ruling emperor.

From early in the third century fine tablewares were made in Britain rather than being imported, some coated with slips of different colours: the London wares from south-east England were grey, while Oxford wares were red to look like Samian pottery – whatever it was that forced Samian out of business, it clearly was not its lack of appeal. Pottery manufacture was big business, on an industrial scale, and wares from big potteries like those in the Nene Valley, from Northampton to the Wash, were widely distributed. Analyzing where some wares have been excavated shows how they were transported: despite the straight well-maintained roads built by the Romans, most pottery probably went by river.

Not all Roman pottery was tableware. A mortarium is a shallow, solid dish used for grinding spices. Grit made from quartz was set in its inside surface to make it suitably rough and abrasive. Amphorae are huge storage vessels, usually sandy-pink and up to a metre (about 3 feet) or more high, with narrow necks and pointed bases. They were used for transporting and storing liquids like wine, olive oil and garum, a strong-smelling fish sauce rather like Worcestershire Sauce.

Kitchenwares for cooking and storage included gritty grey pottery, and rather handsome black-burnished pots. The various sizes, shapes and colours can be seen in this collection from a Roman site at Lower Basildon in Berkshire. It is important to remember that, for all its sophistication, Roman pottery was unglazed, so if anything is glazed it must be medieval or later in date.

processing finds

An important consideration on Roman sites is planning for the variety and quantity of objects the excavation is likely to produce. There should be large supplies of plastic 'finds bags', and trays with labels and waterproof markers to ensure that all items are correctly labelled with the number of the layer or context from which they came. *Time Team* , like many other archaeological teams, relies on willing volunteers to clean objects and make them available to specialists. It is often the first job a person does on an excavation and removing the dirt often produces some of the most exciting discoveries.

Pottery and bone are washed with a toothbrush or small nailbrush and the water is changed frequently, as otherwise it will leave a thin film of mud which will

sorting finds into bags and boxes at York

obscure the surface of the item. A separate rinsing bowl is sometimes used to ensure that the find is clean before it is placed in the drying tray. Although most Roman pottery is well-fired and therefore quite hard and able to withstand vigorous brushing, some Roman wares were coated with a liquid clay or slip which can be removed if they are washed too enthusiastically. It is bad practice to tip bags of finds into water to soften the mud as doing this may also soften less well-fired pieces of pot including prehistoric material, and fragments of wall plaster which may be in the bag. The edges of a pot must be scrupulously clean as these are where the pottery specialist examines the clay from which it was made. Washed pieces of pot are placed in the drying tray on clean newspaper, with a label that duplicates all the information on the finds bag or excavation label.

As well as pottery and bone, some stones and floor and roofing tiles, can be washed and allowed to dry. However, many items can be severely damaged by washing. This is particularly true of metal objects, especially those which might require specialist conservation. Corroded iron and bronze items can decay quickly once they have been excavated and the intricate surface detail on coins and jewellery can be totally lost by rubbing the surface.

Processing finds is a painstaking task which sometimes involves marking the objects with permanent ink – an irritating job which many people try to avoid as the nibs invariably get clogged with clay from the surface of pots. Archaeologists are still searching for a suitable alternative to the traditional dip pens and Indian ink. Some groups of material, like unworked burnt flint which is collected to show possible areas of hearths, is normally counted, weighed and discarded. The remaining finds are catalogued, rebagged and boxed, and are then sent to specialists who examine the collection in detail and provide a detailed report to accompany the site archive or published report.

Phil on... the Romans

I enjoy digging Roman sites, but probably not as much as I enjoy excavating prehistoric ones. My approach to the Romans has always been that they were a bit too much like us and had all the problems we've got. They had inflation, coinage and, even worse, bureaucrats, and laws. All their factory-made pots leave me a bit cold – just the sheer quantity of the stuff. It's a bit wasteful: throw it away and buy a new one – rather like us.

Still, I always get excited about finding pottery because I like finding pottery. Equally, it's one-half of the main information that tells you who the people were that lived on a site, when they lived there and, I guess, what sort of lives they led. Pots are important as dating evidence, which gives a span of occupation. A lot of the pottery is dated in broad terms. Now, broad terms for Romanists can be something like a couple of hundred years, but for someone like me who is usually dealing with the Neolithic or Palaeolithic – by God, if I could be given a date within 200 years! Huh, chance would be a fine thing…

Most of the Roman sites *Time Team* has dug have had stone buildings but this doesn't necessarily mean the Romans only built in stone. It's because we were in areas where the geology was spot on for making stone buildings. When *Time Team* dug at Tockenham and Netheravon in Wiltshire, neither of which are in areas where there is good building stone, the only structural remains we found were a bit of chalk build and a bit of flint build. The most substantial part of the villas on this type of site is usually the roof. The Romans were importing tiles to put on roofs, so there were loads of those. Large parts of the actual fabric of such buildings, like the walls, were made out of clay and daub and stuff like that.

Distinguishing the alignments of walls is one of the keys to determining the various phases of a building. You can tell how a building has been laid out. Looking for phasing is one of the main reasons why digging can't be rushed – you have to systematically plot each bit of masonry on the site plan, lift it up and see how it relates to other walls. One of the things to look for is whether walls are bonded together or whether they butt up against each other. If they're bonded in, they belong to the same phase. If they butt up, one may be later than the other – but that is very much a rule of thumb because you might be looking at the foundations, which were sometimes butted up against each other even though they were built in the same phase. We saw this in the Roman villa at Turkdean in Gloucestershire where the walls were undoubtedly from the same phase, but weren't bonded.

When you are dealing with a villa like the one we dug at Waltham in Gloucestershire, a poorly built wall can look like rubble, which is why it is vitally important to have detailed plans so that you know where each stone was before it was taken off. If you plough through the wall at a later stage and think, 'Oh my God, we've screwed up. We've destroyed a wall!' you've at least got a record of it. You sometimes find floor surfaces between walls. An everyday Romano-British house would probably have a chalk or packed earthern floor. It's only when you get something like the surface we found at Whittington – a really good *opus signinum*, virtually concrete, floor – that you know what you're dealing with.

geophysical survey

A geophysical survey is a bit like X-raying the ground – a variety of techniques can tell archaeologists what lies underneath it even if nothing is visible on the surface. *Time Team* uses three main techniques: magnetometry, resistivity and ground-penetrating radar.

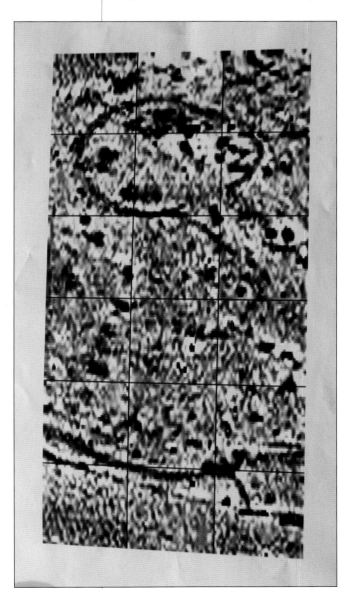

Magnetometry measures differences in the magnetism of the ground just below the surface. Because iron particles become more magnetic when they are burnt, it picks up features like hearths and pottery kilns, and anything built with bricks (which are made from fired clay). It is also good at finding buried ditches. Topsoil is generally more magnetic than subsoils, so a ditch that has been dug into subsoil or bedrock and subsequently filled with topsoil will show up. An iron object, which is very magnetic, appears as a sharp spike in the graph produced by the magnetometer data.

Magnetometry is the quickest of the three geophysical techniques – it is possible to cover as much as 2 hectares (5 acres) in a day and the results can be remarkably clear, as at Tockenham in Wiltshire where the plan of a Roman villa was perfectly reproduced in almost every detail. However, like other geophysical techniques, it is not actually an 'archaeology detecting device' – it simply shows what is under the ground, and readings can be produced by natural changes as well as by archaeology. It can also be affected by any other magnetic material, so anyone operating a magnetometer has to avoid wearing any metal. Zips, glasses and watches must all be plastic; car keys and credit cards (they have a magnetic strip) have to be left behind – and woe betide anyone who turns up wearing an underwired bra!

Resistivity is slower than magnetometry, but is better at picking up buried archaeological features like walls. A machine that looks rather like a Zimmer frame sends an electrical current through the ground from one probe to another and measures the resistance the current meets. The familiar principle that water is a good conductor of electricity means that buried pits or ditches full of moist topsoil will put up little resistance to the current, while drier material such as stone in buried walls will give a high resistance. At Tockenham the resistivity results were so good that we could even see the shape of the rounded end of the Roman dining room.

Ground-penetrating radar (GPR) works by sending radar waves into the ground and measuring the amount of time it takes for them to bounce back. The speed with which they do this depends on the kind of material they are travelling through. For example

John Gater with the geophysics kit at Cirencester

they move at about 15 centimetres (6 inches) every billionth of a second (a nanosecond) in dry sand, but only about 5 centimetres (22 inches) per nanosecond in wet sand. The waves travel even more quickly through air – 30 centimetres (12 inches) per nanosecond – but much more slowly through stone so they can pick up underground voids and walls. The great advantage of GPR is that it can be used when other geophysical techniques cannot. It comes into its own if the target is more than about a metre below the surface – at Papcastle in Cumbria it successfully located Roman wall foundations more than 1.5 metres (5 feet) underground – or when the ground is covered by tarmac or concrete. However, like all geophysical techniques, it simply tells you what is there – the skill comes in interpreting the readings as archaeological features. This can be difficult and on the whole GPR is not widely used in archaeology at present.

Roman Personal Items

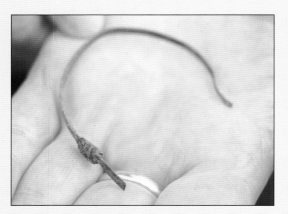

Roman sites are notable for the number of personal items they turn up. This may reflect a higher standard of living than previously, but could also be because jewellery and similar items may have been made of leather or wood in earlier periods and so would tend not to survive into the archaeological record. *Time Team* found the objects shown on a variety of Roman sites. The small bone dice (top left), with the numbers arranged exactly as they are on modern dice, was uncovered at Cirencester, Gloucestershire, along with a gaming piece (above left) in black, red and white glass. These hint at the leisured life led by the rich occupants of the town in the fourth century AD.

Jewellery is a relatively common find. Turkdean in Gloucestershire produced the enamel brooch (below) bearing the message 'utere felix' (be happy) and a tiny copper-alloy bracelet (top right) that would have fitted around a baby's chubby wrist.

One of the most remarkable finds – part of a Roman mirror (right) – came from Papcastle, Cumbria. Amazingly, once it had been treated by a conservation expert it was possible to see a ghostly image in it, even though it had been in the ground for more than 1,600 years. It is items like these that bring to life the people who once lived on an archaeological site.

metal detecting

Metal detecting is a thorny issue for archaeologists. That is because all too often sites are raided by metal-detectors who strip them of crucial finds. There are two points of law here. Firstly, if the finds are taken without the landowner's permission it is theft in the same way that taking something from his house would be. Secondly, the law of 'treasure trove' states that if a find is made of gold or silver, or appears to be, it must be reported to a museum. If this museum, or any other, wishes to aquire it the finder will be compensated for its value. This value is determined by an independent committee.

Even where metal detecting is done within the law, it is all too frequently the case that finds are not recorded properly and any archaeological information is lost. Another problem is that even when items are taken to museums the fact that they were removed from the ground 'unarchaeologically' means that no one has any idea what layer or 'context' they came from. An object may have been the one surviving piece of dating evidence from a ditch-fill and could tell us when an entire villa was built – but if archaeologists don't know that it came from there, the link can never be made.

But responsible archaeological use of metal detectors is possible and can be very useful: on an excavation they can be used to scan spoil heaps as small metal items may be lost during mattocking – when the topsoil is stripped mechanically. However, most metal detectors are used on sites that are not under excavation. Nevertheless, metal detecting can still be very useful to archaeology. If a field has been ploughed, all the finds in the plough soil will already have been ripped from their archaeological context, and in this case, provided the the holes dug to retrieve finds are no more than 15–22 centimetres (6–9 inches) deep and the finds are located, recorded and preserved properly, no further damage will result. The position of each significant find should be plotted as accurately as possible on a plan of the field – ploughing does not normally move items very far, and a concentration of items of a particular date in a particular part of a field may indicate an archaeological site. All finds should be reported to the local museum or county archaeological unit, who will be able to enter details of what they are and where they were found on the county's Sites and Monuments Record.

In many counties excellent metal-detectors are transforming our understanding of the past, identifying many new sites and even showing that parts of the country were occupied much earlier than was previously thought. The villa site that *Time Team* investigated at Lavenham in Suffolk would not have come to the attention of archaeologists without the remarkable number of brooches found by metal detectors.

The army help out with some metal detecting

Roman Inscriptions

The years of the Roman occupation were a literate period, characterised by, among other things, a widely understood alphabet. This in turn led to a custom that was new in Britain: recording events, announcements, gifts and so on as inscriptions carved in stone and displayed on monuments in public places – something that would not be seen again on any scale until the eighteenth and nineteenth centuries.

Many of the stones were broken up in the centuries that followed the Roman occupation, and only fragments have survived. There are very few inscriptions that give dates or name buildings in Roman towns. Whilst some refer to a dedication to a Roman god and others make reference to a patron or emperor, it would be rare to find a piece of stone that stated the name of the building to which it belonged, who built the building and when. That would certainly be every archaeologist's dream!

The letters shown here are part of a larger inscription. This piece was found at Greenwich Park in London. When the letters were analysed, it was revealed to have probably been a dedication to Jupiter and the spirit of the Emperor. This find was instrumental in identifying the building that *Time Team* found as a Roman temple. The inscription also may include the name of the person who commissioned the dedication. Stone was expensive, as was the cost of carving it. The donor who commissioned this inscription must have been able to afford it – and believed that it was a necessary expenditure. Such an inscription would have been a very public way of displaying your wealth and status, as well as your piety and loyalty to the empire.

Inscriptions were not just things for monumental display, but could be found on tombstones, milestones and writing tablets; as graffiti scratched on walls and pottery; or as names on knives or ingots. And there are two general forms of inscription style: formal writing for important messages (as shown in the picture) and cursive writing (which is like spiky disjointed handwriting), used for everyday inscriptions and graffiti. Such evidence provides us with a wonderful source of information about the people of Roman Britain.

Mick on... Roman sites

The Romans would have been the first people in Timechester to produce lasting buildings – there is no real evidence that the prehistoric people who lived in Britain used stone in the way they did. And mortar, plaster and concrete were totally unheard of before the conquest.

Many Roman roads still survive and it is often possible to see that their alignments come up to a town, but not into it. The alignment of the town walls are often visible, as are the main gates – the only entrances to, and exits from, the town. Even where the walls and gates haven't survived, the locations of the latter can still be identified. What is reasonably clear if you look at known plans of the roads inside a town and compare them with what comes later, is that the Roman street plan was often completely trashed. Even in places like Colchester it has been totally replaced. Inside a town's walls there was often what was effectively a total replanning in the Late Saxon period. There are arguments about exactly when this happened, but it basically took place some time between the ninth and eleventh centuries.

The key archaeological question that would need answering at Timechester would be about the transition from the Romans to the Saxons. How long did it remain a Roman town – and in what form? Did it become prosperous again in the eighth or ninth century – or in the tenth, eleventh or twelfth? These are questions that can be applied to all towns: Gloucester, Colchester, London, Winchester.

Timechester in 350 was a society that was totally market-orientated. It used coinage and was plugged into an international economy. This kind of economy brings prosperity but is very vulnerable to outside change because most people rely on the outside world to provide food and other essentials. If the arrangement between townspeople and food producers collapses in any way, the people in towns will starve unless they start farming. I think something like this happened in Britain in the fifth century and the change in the relationship between townspeople and food producers caused a breakdown in the system. Links with the rest of Europe started to fail and, because it was impossible to buy and sell goods, no money was made and the economy collapsed. Although I think this was coupled with a massive plague epidemic which would have greatly affected towns like Timechester, this may not have been the reason they became so decayed. Between one-third and one-half of Britain's population died of the Black Death in the mid-fourteenth century, but society didn't collapse. So it was probably something else that struck the population of Timechester.

The questions to ask at Timechester are similar to the ones *Time Team* asked at Cirencester in Gloucestershire. What was the state of the Roman defences? Is there any indication that Germanic people were invading Britain? The best evidence for an Anglo-Saxon presence would come from burials. Excavations like the one at Dorchester-on-Thames in Oxfordshire reveal a scatter of these. On *Time Team* sites most finds suggest that the Roman way of life lasted for maybe a century longer than is generally thought. This agrees with findings from other excavations – and is contrary to the accepted idea that the Romano-British way of life came to an abrupt end in 410 when the Roman empire washed its hands of Britain.

CHAPTER 6

anglo-saxon

carenza's story of
Timechester in 600

Timechester in 600 looks completely different to the thriving town of 250 years ago. The elegant houses, the paved streets, the mosaics, the fine pottery and the distant well-cultivated farmland have vanished. Instead, there is an irregular cluster of small, thatched huts and animal pens grouped around a handful of timber-framed houses connected by frequently muddy tracks. The settlement is a twentieth of its former size and fields run right up to its edge. Some of the more distant sides of the valley are scrubby pasture, others are covered with trees. Only the town walls remain to remind us that this is the same place, but they are in a sorry state – ruinous and in many places standing only a few stones high. What on earth has happened to Timechester in the last 250 years?

The Roman town flourished for a few decades after 350, but life became more difficult. There was political unrest when the Roman general Magnus Maximus declared himself emperor and sporadic attacks by pirates and raiders from Scotland, Ireland and northern Europe. The people of Timechester, feeling increasingly insecure, hid their coins and valuables in the ground in case they had to leave their comfortable houses in a hurry, and the town council rebuilt and strengthened the town walls. One by one, the legions in Britain were redeployed to defend the heartland of the Roman empire in Italy, southern France and Spain. Rome itself was sacked in 410 so it was hardly surprising that when, in that same year, the British asked – not for the first time – for the legions to return to protect them. The emperor Honorius turned the request down, and told the province it must defend itself.

For a generation the people of Timechester did just that. Life carried on much as before, as the inhabitants of the town tried to maintain the old standards of life, patching up mosaics, for example, and keeping the water supply running. But law and order was breaking down everywhere as people, including runaway slaves, realized that there were rich pickings to be made from banditry and looting. Cross-country travel became increasingly risky, which had a catastrophic effect on Timechester where so many people made their livings by producing goods for trade and where public building and the salaries of local administrators were paid for by taxes on the marketplace. With fewer and fewer traders coming to the market, there was little money to be made. Nevertheless, the town was still comparatively prosperous and there was the nagging fear that this might make it a special target for looting. Some families left Timechester, taking only their portable valuables with them. Most of them headed for Wales where it was said that Romanized Christian communities still lived in security and comfort. A few mercenaries from Europe arrived and they stayed on, promising to support the citizens of Timechester and defend the area by force if necessary. This seemed to be an extreme measure in Timechester, where law-abiding members of the community had never needed to resort to arms – but times had changed.

Life had also changed in the surrounding countryside. The slaves at Upchester villa were freed so that they would remain loyal, but many left the valley and there was no one to bring them back. With no market for the grain the villa produced, there was no money to pay farm workers, and certainly none to spend on maintaining the villa buildings. Deprived of their livelihood, craftsmen such as potters and mosaic-makers had to turn to farming. They paid for the right to cultivate some of the villa's land for themselves by helping out on the rest and the owners of the villa were therefore able to keep the estate, the hallmark of Roman respectability, largely intact. However, their position was precarious and eventually the villa was attacked by bandits. Its buildings were looted and the servants were clubbed to death and thrown down the only working well. The villa owner and his family fled.

No one reoccupied such an unlucky site: there was no need. The population of the Timechester area dropped rapidly as their poor diet and living conditions made people, particularly children, vulnerable to disease and injury. Everyone was wary of starting a family which they feared would not survive. With no market and the demand for food falling, fewer fields were cultivated each year and the poorest land began to revert to scrub.

In 446 an outbreak of plague left just four families in Timechester – fewer people caught the disease in the surrounding countryside, where the population was more dispersed. By the end of the fifth century AD much of Timechester itself lay empty: only about seventy people remained. The community gained some reassurance from the encircling town walls although it lacked the resources to maintain them properly. Upkeep of the elegant town houses was out of the question and these gradually fell into disrepair as, one after another, roofs fell in leaving the walls to crumble. Grass grew on the Roman road and one day the central arch of the bridge fell through. Thereafter the river had to be waded across, a risky business when it was in flood. Smaller wooden houses were built, some in the ruins of the former buildings. Where possible these made use of walls that were still standing, but the old footings could get in the way and soon it became easier to build from scratch. Only the ruins of stone buildings distinguished the former town from the increasingly thinly populated countryside.

The emptying countryside around Timechester proved attractive to Saxons from the North Sea coastal regions of Germany, who were themselves being attacked by other tribes that were sweeping across Europe. Some came as aggressors, but others just wanted somewhere to live and claimed that they were related to the mercenaries who had helped defend the town three generations earlier. They camped in and around the abandoned villa ruins at Upchester and built wooden houses there over time. This small settlement came to be known as Sutton, as it lay south of Timechester. A cluster of ancient grassy mounds on the nearby hillside reminded them of the burial grounds in their homelands and they chose to bury their dead there, far from the Roman cemetery just outside Timechester's crumbling walls.

More continental newcomers arrived in the valley over the years but kept themselves apart from the suspicious Britons who remained in the area. These Saxons built farmsteads scattered across the countryside, and the head of the family at Sutton declared himself their leader. Their way of life was very different to that of the Britons. For example, although they made coarse pottery tempered with grass, wooden or leather vessels were more often used for cooking and storage. They wore brightly checked, roughly woven clothes fastened with ornate brooches and worshipped new, violent gods. The Saxons revered their weapons, and their dead were buried fully dressed and accompanied by the items they had treasured in life.

Those who felt threatened by these new ways moved away from Timechester to regions where they could maintain their identity by speaking their own language, and made futile attempts to resist the Saxon tide by force. But others remained and farmed alongside the new arrivals. For them it was a relief to abandon the Christian god, who seemed to have let them down, and they turned instead to the pagan gods of the Saxons. Soon everyone in and around Timechester, whatever their ethnic origin, was wearing Saxon clothing and jewellery and using the newcomers' weapons and language.

By 600 the fertile Time Valley around Timechester contained ten small settlements, each containing just a few buildings housing the members of one or two extended families. The biggest of the settlements was still within the ruined

walls of Timechester, but even this had room for only six families and contained no more than twenty buildings. The largest was the chief's hall, which was surrounded by haystacks, pens and small paddocks for animals, and by several smaller timber buildings that were used for storing food or for craft activities such as weaving. Clustered around the hall were the smaller houses of other families, which were also surrounded by paddocks and huts. Food was rarely plentiful: porridge or bread made from wheat, rye, peas or oats grown in the fields around each settlement formed the monotonous bulk of most meals. Pigs, cows, sheep and goats were well tended, but meat was generally reserved for special occasions. However, beer brewed from barley was drunk with

most meals. Although life was not easy, there were occasional feasts when everyone congregated in the chief's house and listened to legends that told how invasion and conquest, fighting and famine, death and disease had been experienced just a few generations earlier. Most of the enthralled listeners were pleased that they were living in their own time, and not that of their ancestors.

historical evidence

Historical or written evidence can be divided into two types. First, there are primary sources, which are mainly official documents and include well-known examples of national importance such as *Magna Carta*, the charter granted by King John in 1215, which recognized the rights and privileges of England's barons, churchmen and freemen. These provide much of our knowledge of political history, national events and the succession of the monarchy. More useful to archaeologists are documents such as wills, manorial court records, inquests, taxation returns, censuses and so on. These cover specific places and contain information about everyday life. *Domesday Book*, a unique document that dates to 1086, was commissioned by William the Conqueror, and is a survey of the country he had taken over. It records all England in great detail – estates are described down to the number of mills, ploughed fields and even pigs. It also shows how most of them had been taken from the Anglo-Saxon lords and given instead to French soldiers and William's relatives.

The other class of historical records is secondary sources, written about events that befell others. For example, Tacitus, a Roman historian, wrote about the Roman conquest of Britain; in *The Ruin of Britain* Gildas, a monk writing in Wales in the middle of the sixth century AD, tells of hordes of heathen barbarians killing Romanized Britons; and in the eighth century another monk, Bede, wrote a history of the English Church that covered many political events and is renowned as the first history of England. Another famous document is the *Anglo-Saxon Chronicle*, which records events from AD 1 until 1154.

University libraries are a great help in gaining access to information, but local libraries can also obtain most secondary sources published in English. The best results are likely to come from local County Records Offices, which will hold a range of local-interest books and original documents, including maps, that can date back as far as the medieval period and cover areas ranging in size from one farm to an entire county. In addition, some county historical societies publish historical records in the form of small books which cover anything from details of medieval taxpayers to contemporary diaries, and may well include both primary and secondary records.

The Public Record Office at Kew near London holds original copies of many unpublished exchequer documents that are not accessible anywhere else. However, understanding, or even reading, original documents can be impossible without historical training, and most archaeologists ask a specialist to do this work.

Using information from sources like these, archaeologists can put together an outline history of a place although they need to be on their guard – historical evidence is rarely as straightforward as it may seem. Official records were not written with archaeologists' requirements in mind and do not include all the information that they want. Also, they may not be accurate – for example, tax lists will not include people who avoided paying, and the authors of many secondary sources had their own agendas, which could severely bias their record of events. Gildas's *The Ruin of Britain* is in fact a long sermon encouraging people to return to a pious Christian life, in which he depicts the Saxon invasions as a punishment for ungodly living. Given this perspective, it was in his interest to describe them as bloodthirstily as possible.

Historical evidence is very thin for the Anglo-Saxon period: writing things down was one of the traditions of Roman life that was abandoned when people had to concentrate on day-to-day survival. However, from the medieval period onwards most places will have some documented history.

Saxon Brooch

Saxon brooches are generally found in female graves – men were usually interred with items such as swords and shields – and this one was probably pinned to the dress the dead woman wore when she was buried. Because it had been in the ground for centuries it was covered in clay from the surrounding grave fill and encrusted with rust and other deposits that formed as the body decomposed. Where the surface could be seen it was a dull greyish-green with little sign of decoration.

However, now the brooch has been carefully cleaned and examined in minute detail, it is possible to get an idea of what it would have looked like when it was new. It is made of bronze, which tarnishes and goes green if it is not cleaned. In fact, it is also gilded, a process that would have helped to prevent the bronze tarnishing and kept it bright and shiny. X-rays of the brooch showed that there was more decoration than was immediately visible beneath the debris and corrosion – a delicate design of dots and circles adorned the area between the outer edge and the centre. They also show that the rust on its back was actually the remains of the pin, which had a loop at one end where it was attached to the brooch.

This is a fairly ordinary piece of jewellery – pretty, shiny and made with a certain amount of care, but not especially ornate. It is a practical item

that held the wearer's clothing together, but had clearly been designed to look attractive. Although life was not particularly comfortable during the Anglo-Saxon period, people nevertheless enjoyed owning nice things and the many personal items, such as combs and tweezers, that tend to turn up on archaeological sites suggest that they were concerned about their appearance.

Most Anglo-Saxon brooches are found in graves and some very ornate gold ones have been uncovered. These are in the shape of crosses with huge square heads or decorations of interlocking squares, circles, triangles, spirals and sometimes even stylized animals. The designs are picked out with gold wire and set with shaped red and gold garnets, white shells and blue or green glass. Graves with brooches like these often contain other ornate items such as rings and bead necklaces of amethyst, crystal and amber. Such objects must have been highly valued, and it seems strange to us that they were buried with the dead, rather than being handed down from generation to generation.

excavating graves

Archaeologists often know in advance if they are likely to find human graves. The Bronze Age tradition of burial under, or adjacent to, large man-made mounds or barrows makes grave sites of this period highly visible in the landscape. Roman urban cemeteries are invariably just outside the town walls alongside roads leading out of the settlement. In the Christian tradition the requirement for burial to take place in hallowed ground means that the location of most cemeteries from the medieval period onwards is known. When excavating a grave in one of these sites it is necessary to obtain a Home Office licence – this legislation was introduced in the nineteenth century to prevent bodysnatching for financial gain. But the sites of burial places of other religions from other periods, are likely to be forgotten, and a grave can turn up unexpectedly on a dig. In this case the coroner must be informed before a licence to dig can be obtained.

In his protective clothing, phil excavating a skeleton at Launceston

The first sign of a grave, which usually appears when a trench is being trowelled clean, is a narrow rectangular patch that looks or feels different to the surrounding surface. Its size varies depending on the size of the person it was dug for, but most are between 1 and 2 metres (about 3 and 6 feet) long and 50 centimetres (20 inches) to 1 metre (3 feet) wide. Once the outline has been plotted, the diggers start taking out the grave fill, keeping a careful eye out for any finds. These can be tiny – shroud pins, for example, are little bigger than modern sewing pins and are very easy to miss.

Unless the soil is very acidic, in which case only a few teeth may survive, an archaeologist will expect to find bones. If the grave has been undisturbed the first bone that is uncovered is likely to be the skull as its rounded shape will stand proud of the rest of the skeleton. When such remains are discovered, Home Office regulations stipulate that they must be screened from public view to give them the respect due to them as the bones of a human being. It is important to wear a protective suit and mask when excavating the remains or the skeleton may be infected with flakes of skin, drops of sweat and so on.

Because bone is so delicate, the best way to excavate is to trowel to just above the skeleton, and then pick off the rest of the grave fill with more delicate instruments, such as small leaf-trowels, wooden spatulas, brushes and even dental picks. Hands and feet are particularly difficult because the bones are tiny and it is fiddly to clean around them. Archaeologists do not try to remove absolutely every last grain of dirt – just enough to show how the skeleton is lying in the grave.

If a burial dates from the Anglo-Saxon or Bronze Age periods there is a chance that the grave will contain items buried with the deceased. These could include jewellery, weapons or the remains of food. Archaeologists try to interpret these as best

Anglo-Saxon Pottery

This Saxon pottery shows many of the characteristics that are typical of pottery made in England between about 450 and 850. Although it may not seem very beautiful to us today, without finds like this we would know virtually nothing about Anglo-Saxon daily life. Its importance is highlighted by the fact that, because pottery does not seem to have been made in much of the west and north of Britain, hardly anything is known about how people in lived in that part of the country.

These fragments would have been part of a small round pot which could have been used for cooking, or for storing food such as butter, curd cheese, nuts or flour. It was made of clay and would have been fashioned by hand – mass-production of wheel-thrown pottery ended when the Romans left Britain. Pots and bowls were shaped in one of two ways. The clay was either moulded or it was rolled out to form thin 'snakes', which were coiled in a rising spiral. The joins between the coils were then smoothed over. Although pots like this were sometimes burnished with a smooth pebble to make the surface shiny, they are seldom decorated. They were not glazed, so would not have been waterproof.

The clay used in the pot would have been tempered with grass and chaff to prevent it breaking during firing, which was done quite simply in a fire in a hollow in the ground. This was covered with turf to keep the heat in and the high temperature burnt away the grass and chaff, leaving small hollows in the sides of the pot.

For more than 300 years pots remained unchanged. The only ones that were different were those that were filled with the ashes of cremated bodies and then buried. These were larger than cooking and storage pots and were usually decorated with scratched lines, round or square stamps, or pieces of clay. Some are incredibly ornate while others have just a few lines around their necks. Ashes were also buried in plain pots, possibly because the family of the person who had died could not afford a decorated one or, of course, as a matter of personal preference.

The remains of everyday pottery are the best indication of a possible Anglo-Saxon settlement: wooden structures rot and post holes can be difficult to see. The best way to proceed on a likely site is to methodically scour ploughed fields for pottery fragments – although this, too, is not easy as the pieces of pot do not stand out very well in the soil.

they can – jewellery can be seen as evidence of the person's wealth, weapons might show their role in society and food could be for his or her journey into the afterlife – but it is impossible to know for sure.

Once the skeleton has been uncovered as completely as possible, it is photographed from above and a plan is drawn. It is important to make sure that the direction in which the body is lying is clearly indicated, as Christian burials are almost invariably orientated east–west, with the head at the west end of the grave.

The bones are then carefully removed and transferred to boxes where they are maintained in acid-free conditions. After they have been analyzed, and a record made of any evidence of the skeleton's age, sex, life history and any diseases the person may have suffered, the bones will usually be retained by a museum, or reinterred.

Phil on... the Anglo-Saxons

Anglo-Saxon archaeology is very much about bodies – the Anglo-Saxons never lived, but always died! Digging skeletons, apart from your brindled Iron Age ones, is pretty straightforward once you know the technique. When I dug my first one I'd never seen such a ham-fisted piece of excavation in all my life. And it took me about three days to do it. Now it's like falling off a log. For the most part, the skeletons are very predictable, because you know that the head is going to be attached to the shoulders, and the shoulders are going to be attached to the arms, and the leg bone will be attached the ankle bone, and the ankle bone attached to the foot bone, now hear the word of the Lord … So you know where everything is going to be.

I struggle to find Saxon settlement sites because they are quite rare and difficult to locate (I dug one only last winter though, a cracker). They've got big buildings shown by big post holes. The last time I saw structures like these was near Petersfield in Hampshire where there were these glorious large timber halls. We just stripped off the area and then got far enough back and high enough up to look down and see whacking great big oblongs of posts, with opposing doorways. The halls were like the ones described in the Viking sagas. They were just absolutely magnificent. It was a stunning site. If I had

to choose any house from any period of history to live in, I would probably pick a nice big Saxon hall. They were very noble structures, with lots of people in them. And you would have had to drink lots of beer in them!

There were no finds at the Petersfield site because the Anglo-Saxons dug a hole, they put a post in and then the dirt went straight back in again. There really wasn't that much opportunity for material to get worked in with it. Also, because Saxon pottery was very lowly fired, any pots on the site wouldn' t have survived the ploughing.

Most Saxon sites are what we now call sunken featured buildings (SFBs) – people still like to call them 'grubs' after the old term *grubenhaūs* – and not halls. SFBs are lovely little things, usually with a lot of stuff in them, particularly pottery and loom weights. The beauty of a Saxon site is that if an area is big enough, and you can get far enough away from it, it is actually possible to see the whole layout of a settlement.

Winterbourne Gunner in Wiltshire was a Saxon site on chalk and illustrated why I like excavating on chalk – everything stood out clearly and it confirmed the textbook opinion that it is one of the nicest soils to dig on. When you get nice chalk, there ain't nothing better. Once you've dug on it, you're a bit spoilt for anything else. However, digging on pasty, decayed chalk is horrible. You've got to be something of a geologist, because it's necessary to know what the soils are doing and how they got there.

I like Saxon sites because effectively they're the first English settlements and come from a time when England was my kind of nation. And I love the Saxons. I suppose it' s easy to think that they were a bit crude and hairy, attacking each other with axes and double-handed broadswords, but when you see the quality of some of their artwork and metalwork you see that they were stunning, sophisticated people. I've got a lot of time for them.

timber buildings

Wooden buildings were very common in the past, and were built in many different ways. The Anglo-Saxon *grubenhaüs*, or sunken featured building, is one of the simplest types. It was made by setting two posts into the ground, 3 or 4 metres (10 to 13 feet) apart, in holes packed with stones to wedge them upright. The posts probably supported either end of a horizontal pole that held up a pitched roof covered with thatch or turf. The floor inside the building was hollowed out. A wooden floor was probably laid across the hollow and must have improved drainage. On a dry site, sunken featured buildings show up as a rough, rectangular depression, rarely deeper than 1 metre (3 feet), with a post hole (not always packed with stones) at either end.

Many other Anglo-Saxon buildings, as well as later and Roman constructions, were rectangular timber-framed structures, much larger than a *grubenhaüs*. These could be built by setting the upright posts directly into the ground, either in post holes or in a trench, but it was more common for a horizontal sill-beam to be used as a foundation. This was sometimes placed in a trench, to stop it shifting, or it was kept above ground and rested on a low stone wall, which kept the timber dry and helped to stop it rotting. In an archaeological excavation it should be possible to see any foundation trenches, or the stone walls. In another form of construction the timber frame rested on a number of stone post-pads piled on top of each other – useful if you want a structure that is raised above the ground. These large stones, which stood above ground level, kept the building dry and could be used to store food, like a granary. A larger flat stone on top of these pads, creating an overhang, could keep the rats out.

The kind of simple round house that was common in Iron Age settlements had a curving wall comprised of a circle of posts set into the ground and interwoven with thin flexible branches covered by a thatch- or turf-covered conical roof. On a dry site, the only trace that will survive are the post holes, with their packing of stones. These may be a circle of individual holes packed with stones, or a continuous curving trench with a gap where the doorway was.

Many styles of timber building leave very little archaeological trace. If the wood rots away the empty foundation trenches and post holes are easily destroyed by later occupation or ploughing and, even if they do survive, can be very difficult to see during excavation. And that assumes the builders did actually dig into the ground. If wooden sleeper beams that rested on the ground have disappeared, the only indication that they existed might be a line of pebbles that were kicked against them before they rotted. It is a sobering thought that most timber buildings probably leave no archaeological trace at all.

DNA analysis

With the cracking of the human genome making big headlines in 2000, it might seem that DNA holds the solution to every problem. But, as in tackling disease, the use of DNA analysis in archaeology is still in its infancy. Its potential is huge, but its application so far has been limited.

Most archaeological DNA work to date has concentrated on human remains, although markers have been identified that can differentiate between animal species like sheep and goat, horse and mule – it is almost impossible to tell them apart just by looking at their bones.

A tooth is the best part of the human skeleton to use for DNA analysis because it is the ideal capsule in which the DNA is preserved. Only a tiny sample is needed, so the first step is to is drill a small hole in the tooth. This is not a job for anyone with a phobia about dentists: the hole must go deep into the root canal, and the smell of burning tooth is much worse than it is in a dental surgery (where water is sprayed on to minimize the smell). Once in the root cavity, it is necessary to recover anything that is there, including the remains of blood vessels. This all emerges as a fine powder, which is dissolved in a series of solvents to break open the cells and release the DNA. The end result is a solution of a few billionths of a gram of DNA in pure water.

A process known as polymerase chain reaction (PCR for short) is then used to amplify the particular bit of the DNA chain the archaeologist is interested in. At Bawsey in Norfolk, for example, *Time Team* wanted to know the sex of the skeleton of someone who had been murdered so the section containing the 'x' and 'y' sex chromosomes was chosen for amplification. Males have both, while females only have 'x' chromosomes. After the PCR it is possible to see the DNA with the naked eye and an electrical current is passed through the sample which sorts it into bands of different chromosomes. If the Bawsey sample had been from a male, there would have been two bands, one of 'x' chromosomes and one of 'y' ones, but there was just the one band, of 'x' chromosomes – so we now know that our murder victim was a woman.

In archaeology DNA analysis is used to identify the sex of children (which is very difficult from visual inspection alone), diseases such as plague, leprosy and syphilis, and congenital conditions such as cystic fibrosis and Down's syndrome. It can also tell whether groups of individuals are related to one another. This sort of information, if widely available, could transform our understanding of the past. It could tell us, for example, whether or not the wealth and status implied by rich burials was inherited and kept within a few elite families. Knowing more about the incidence of diseases in the past could ascertain the impact of measles in the colonization of South America, and tell us what percentage of the fourteenth-century population of Britain was killed by the Black Death – or why leprosy died out so suddenly at about the same time. Understanding when and where particular cancers became prevalent might even help to prevent or treat the disease in the future.

But there are problems with archaeological DNA analysis, not least that DNA does not always survive very well and, generally speaking, the older the sample the worse the problem. Usually, the best that can reasonably be hoped for from, say, a Saxon cemetery in alkaline soils is that about 60 per cent of samples will produce results. In acid soils nothing at all might survive, even from quite a recent burial. The final problem is cost: DNA analysis works out at about £300 per sample, and if a large cemetery is being excavated using it can quickly become prohibitively expensive. Hopefully, such a useful technique may one day be more affordable.

Loom Weight

A loom weight is another find that is characteristic of the Anglo-Saxon period. Weaving was a basic household task and most homes had a loom for making cloth, usually by spinning sheep's wool into threads and then weaving the threads to make fabric.

The loom was an upright wooden frame and the warp or lengthwise threads were draped over it. Cloth was made by weaving the crosswise weft, or woof, threads in and out of the warp ones, which had to be under tension, but fairly flexible. In the Anglo-Saxon period (as in the Neolithic and Bronze Ages) this tension was created by tying handfuls of warp threads around heavy weights. All of these had to weigh roughly the same or one part of the cloth would be more loosely woven than the rest of the fabric and more prone to wear out or fall apart.

One of the easiest ways to ensure a consistent weave was to make equal-sized, and therefore equally heavy, weights from clay. Each one had a hole pierced in it and was smoothed to remove any sharp edges that might cut the threads. The weights were then fired and cooled. Perhaps surprisingly, the shape of loom weights changed over time. Until the middle of the seventh century they were were flat rings, but later in the Anglo-Saxon period they tend to be shaped more like hemispheres. In time, weights went out of use, and medieval manuscripts show women working at looms tensioned by a single wooden beam to which all the warp threads are tied.

Rows of loom weights and sometimes post holes have been found on sites, suggesting the loom was set like the one shown on Victor's picture of the Iron Age period, the design of which continued into the Saxon period. This arrangement is probably the result of a loom being burnt – presumably by accident – because if the weaving had been finished the weights would have been cut off the threads and stowed away for reuse. Such accidents would have meant the waste of a lot of hard work and the loss of a new item of clothing.

osteoarchaeology

Human burials are regularly found during excavations and the skeleton is usually all that is left; only in exceptional circumstances, such as intensely dry or wet conditions, are there any other remains like skin and hair. The archaeologist or scientist therefore has only bones – often poorly preserved and so badly affected by soil conditions that not all of them have survived – to tell him or her about the people of the past. In addition, only certain aspects of a person can be learnt from his or her skeleton.

Standard measurements and features derived from modern-day bodies can be applied to earlier skeletons. Thus it is usually possible to work out the height of the individual from the long leg bones and we can judge how robust or gracile the person was – whether they were heavily or lightly built. Some idea of sex can normally be gained, especially from the form of the hip bones and, less reliably, from the skull. The hips of a female skeleton are wider and more open, to accommodate the growth and birth of babies; they can even show whether the woman has had children or not. A male skull has more dominant brow ridges, a more pronounced zygomatic arch (the cheek bones) and a generally heavier appearance than a female one.

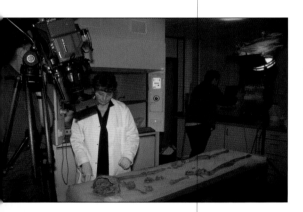

The bones from Bawsey being examined in the laboratory at Bournemouth University

When it comes to estimating the age of the person at death much can be suggested from what is known of growth patterns in children and adolescents, and the changes that occur with aging. As children grow, the bones in their skulls gradually fuse together, as do the epiphyses (the ends) of the long bones in their arms and legs. So it is generally possible to determine the age of a child's skeleton (though not its sex) and the development of the development of the skeleton during adolescence. Once adulthood is reached there are several decades when it is difficult to judge age accurately – one useful way of doing this is to examine the teeth in detail. When estimating age it is necessary to remember that a great deal depends on diet, health, age of onset of puberty and how hard a person worked during their lifetime.

The skeleton can reveal a considerable amount about a person's age (at death) and their stature, build and sex, but what of their life? Although many diseases do not leave any trace some do – spina bifida, tuberculosis, leprosy and syphilis are examples. It is also possible to see the results of deficiency diseases like rickets and, of course, any broken (and healed) bones. In addition, there are certain conditions like DISH (diffuse idiopathic skeleton hyperostosis) which the living person would hardly be aware of, but which indicate an indolent lifestyle with rich food.

Much can therefore be learnt from a close visual inspection of the skeleton, combined with good medical and anatomical knowledge; even more can be learnt when scientific and laboratory research such as DNA analysis is conducted.

Mick on... Anglo-Saxon sites

I keep hoping for a 'grub hut', a sunken featured building (SFB), on a *Time Team* dig, but in general we have found very little from the Saxon period. We uncovered post holes, a hearth and ditches – the remains of a grub – at Kemerton in Worcestershire, but I would have thought that a site like that, which had been occupied for thousands of years, might have produced one or two of these buildings. If a geophysics survey ever indicated the possibility of an SFB we would look for it, no matter what period the site was supposed to be.

The Saxon and medieval periods would have had the most impact on the landscape around Timechester and on the town itself. I always think that to understand why people in modern Britain live in the kind of places they do you have to go back to the settlements that developed then. There were clearly earlier ones but the critical period for the creation of the English village with its hamlets and farmsteads was between the eighth and twelfth centuries. Similarly, whatever towns had been like in Roman times, they had a new beginning in the Middle or Late Saxon period, or were newly founded in the twelfth and thirteenth centuries. So in many towns today the location of the centre and of churches, castles, monasteries – and everything connected with them – dates from then. The buildings of a town like Timechester will be very largely eighteenth, nineteenth and twentieth-century and until the disruptions caused by developers in the late twentieth century, its layout – street pattern, property boundaries and the line of the town wall, all of which relate to topographical features – would have been based on the Saxon and medieval one.

In the early part of the Saxon period towns like Timechester were settlements surrounding the large timber hall of the local chief – and it is places like these that Christian missionaries would have visited in their search for converts. It's easy to imagine that Timechester was visited at this time by a Mercian monk called Eggberg who would later be acclaimed as a saint. Shrines were often erected to these 'holy men' after their deaths and their bones ultimately became relics and points of pilgrimage. Later in the Saxon period, under Alfred the Great, about thirty new Saxon towns were laid out as fortified centres, or burhs. After the Norman Conquest these centres became medieval towns and the shrines of saints developed into parish churches.

If I could visit any period, rather than live in it, it would have to be Late Saxon. I would want to drop in some time around 900 to see what was happening. My interest would be in finding out how a town or village like Oxford, that dates from that time, started. It is reasonably clear that most places that go back to the Roman occupation, such as Circencester, were originally forts. The decision to put one on a particular site was made by a Roman officer and when the legionaries moved on they left behind camp followers who established a settlement that later developed into a town or village. Similarly, we can be reasonably clear about what happened in the twelfth and thirteenth centuries: the lord of a manor had to pay the king for any markets or fairs on the land he held and to raise the money he would lay out burgages and get rent for them. The question is: how does a Saxon chief take a fairly undeveloped place like Oxford and lay out the streets and populate it? Where did the people come from? And what was the incentive for them to settle there?

high medieval

carenza's story of timechester in 1250

More than 600 years have passed since we last looked at Timechester and once again it seems very different although, as before, some slight traces of past activity remain and have influenced the landscape's development. Most strikingly, the town itself is bustling again although it is different in many ways to Roman Timechester. The bridge has been rebuilt, as have the walls, partly reusing the lines of the Roman ones. The main street, which goes from one town gate to the other, is on roughly the same alignment as the Roman main street and leads to a marketplace in the centre of the town. But the layout is different – instead of the gridded Roman plan, long narrow properties run at right angles from both sides of the single central street. The houses are two storeys high and regularly planned but are packed tightly against one another. Behind them are long thin yards containing animal pens, rubbish tips and workshops. On the far side of the street these extend back for 50 metres (165 feet), but on the near side they have been fitted around the edge of a completely new building: a huge castle set on a high mound which takes up much of this end of the town. Another building which has appeared since 600 is the church, positioned along one side of the marketplace. Outside the town, which is spilling beyond the confines of the walls as suburbs begin to develop, the countryside is once again being extensively cultivated. Huge open fields divided into long narrow curving strips are eroding the remains of the Iron Age and Roman field banks. Only patches of woodland and the very tops of the hills are not under the plough, leaving the remains of earlier monuments under pastures grazed by sheep. Timechester occupies a prime location close to the sea and the river is much busier: it is navigable, and ships are moored against the jetties while others are being built or repaired. Sutton, the site where Upchester villa once stood, is now the site of a small village. What has happened since 600 to bring Timechester to bustling life?

At the start of the seventh century Timechester was actually on the verge of great change. The relative peace and stability its occupants enjoyed was in part because the numerous small warring chiefdoms in the region had combined to form a number of larger kingdoms with each chief owing allegiance to his king. Raiding was reduced as the king maintained some degree of law and order which was enforced by his chiefs or thegns. Within half a century a missionary named Eggberg arrived in the Time Valley. He preached the benefits of Christianity over the Anglo-Saxon pagan gods, having recently converted the king to Christianity. The thegn of Timechester was a shrewd man who realized that it would be to his advantage to adopt the new religion if his king had already done so. At first he had a room next to his hall blessed as a shrine to Eggberg (who was made a saint when he died, shortly after leaving Timechester). Within a few generations it became clear that this was not enough and he decided to erect a special building: a church. The space he chose for

this was an empty plot of land near his hall and he dedicated the church, which was built of wood, to St Mary the Virgin. His people had, as a matter of course, converted when he did, but although some adopted the Christian tradition of burial with no grave goods, for several generations others continued to send the dead on their way with offerings placed in graves dug near the barrows at Timebury. This gradually fell out of use as more and more people opted for the convenience of the Christian graveyard around the new church.

The next thegn in Timechester was as receptive to new ideas as his predecessor had been. Aware of the town's good location conveniently close to the sea but not so close as to be too vulnerable to pirate raids, he encouraged its development into a trading port or wic and laid out streets and workshops along the main street. This had remained in use as the most convenient route between the Roman town gates, although the walls were still in ruins. From about 700 Timechester Wic expanded as merchandise from Europe was traded for goods made in the town's workshops. The settlement became densely packed, and by the end of the century the first coins to appear in the Time Valley since the Roman period were in use. But the good times were not to last. In the following century repeated raids by Vikings, aware of the unusual wealth of this settlement in an otherwise rural landscape, caused trade to decline and much of the activity ceased.

The Medieval wall is still visible in the North Wales town of Conwy

In about 890 the town was refortified in response to the raids and, despite occasional sightings of Viking warships along the coast, Timechester itself was attacked only once. Some people had thought Timebury hillfort should be chosen as the site to defend as it was the best place to retreat to, but the decision to choose Timechester paid off: the secured town began to attract trade and craftsmen again and expanded in size. By 1000 the settlement inside the still-visible Roman walls had become a small town.

Equally revolutionary changes were affecting the countryside around Timechester. The valley – a huge estate whose boundaries had changed little since the Roman conquest – was divided up into two smaller units so that the two sons of a local lord could have their own land. The old division between Timechester and Timebury, on either side of the river, had been reinvented. The town of Timechester now owned less farmland but many of its inhabitants, in particular craftsmen and traders, did not have much time to farm and could barter the goods they made or services they provided for food from the rural manor of Timebury. Most were content to keep just a few animals and plant vegetables in the yards behind their houses.

The system of scattered farmsteads and small settlements, each with its own set of paddocks and small arable fields surrounded by pasture, had worked well while the population's demand for land and grain was low. But as the generations came and went in the ninth century the increasing need for grain to feed the expanding town meant that more and more land was brought into cultivation, much of it for the first time since the Roman period. By about 900 there was no longer any land that could be used for arable farming without leaving the sheep and cattle with nowhere to graze – and the animals' manure was needed to fertilize the land.

Over fifty years or so, yields began to drop as crops were grown year after year on the same fields, draining it of nutrients and vital minerals. But lords in other parts of the country had heard of a way to solve the problem. Although drastic, the solution was said to be very effective and in about 950 the lord of Sutton and the peasants farming the land agreed that it should be tried. One winter all the small fields were amalgamated into two vast prairie-like areas, one of which would be cultivated each year while the other lay fallow to be grazed on by animals whose manure would restore the soil. Each field was divided into long thin strips which were allocated to the lord and to each peasant family according to their status. Each family had land in each of the two fields, which they farmed themselves, but the pasture and meadow were common land, for everyone to use. There was now no room for individual farms and paddocks and the small farmsteads were swept away and replaced by a new village at Sutton, close to the lord's house and his small chapel. Sutton village was laid out on a regular plan with houses on either side of the street. Making the change had been a massive undertaking, but it rapidly paid off as crop yields rose to higher levels than ever before.

By 1066, when William of Normandy invaded England and became king after the death of Harold at Hastings, Timechester was a thriving town with several churches. Its overlord had been the king himself. Such a place – prosperous and strategically sited – was clearly one that William the Conqueror did not want to fall into the hands of anyone he could not trust. He gave the overlordship of Timechester to one of his loyal French relations; Sutton he allocated to a follower who had helped him fight for the English crown. To secure such an important holding as Timechester, he promptly had a large timber castle built in one corner of the town. There was no space for such a huge edifice and at least twenty houses had to be knocked down to make way for it. The inhabitants of Timechester were ruefully aware of how powerful their new king was, and how ruthless he could be. Within a few decades, however, placatory gestures had been made and St Mary's church was rebuilt in stone and considerably enlarged.

The next couple of centuries were good times for the Time Valley. The cloth, shoes, pottery and myriad other items produced by craftsmen and sold in the market made good profits and this wealth was used to build other churches, until the laws governing their foundation were changed in the middle of the twelfth century. However, discontent was growing over the high levels of taxes, rents and tolls taken by the lord of Timechester. The townspeople were able to escape these burdens when the lord of the urban manor died in battle in 1230 and left the lordship to his inexperienced sixteen-year-old son. The townspeople petitioned the king for a charter that would allow them their independence from the lord. When this was granted the celebrations lasted for days. It was soon decided that Timechester's new independent status should be marked by building a wall around it – the ultimate sign that a medieval town was doing well. Work soon began and by 1240 the new wall followed much of the course of the old Roman one, fragments of which were still visible.

A constant trickle of new people coming to live and work in Timechester meant that it soon spilled out beyond the wall and houses were built along the roads that led into the town. They were erected on vacant land which had once been used for farming but was now more valuable as sites for housing. But the most sought-after buildings were inside the town wall, where taxes were lower – and those in the main street or marketplace were the best of all. Vacant spaces between buildings along the main street became a distant memory as new structures were crammed into the Late Saxon plots, most of which were divided in half to allow the greatest number of all-important frontages, where goods could be sold, to be on the street.

In the countryside grain yields stayed high, supporting a population that was growing rapidly. The carefully laid-out strip fields mellowed to gentle curving shapes as years of turning the ploughs pulled by ox teams made the strips curve to the left at each end. Gradually too, low ridges built up as the soil was repeatedly turned to the centre of each strip. Ploughing in the opposite direction would have prevented this, but the ridges helped to drain the soil and kept its depth high, which encouraged the valuable crops to grow. In about 1200 a fire destroyed part of the village at Sutton and it was replanned and rebuilt as a miniature replica of a town. Its central street had large regularly laid-out house plots on either either side with backyards containing chickens, pigs, goats, vegetable plots, rubbish tips and ramshackle sheds.

More Anglo-saxons arrived over the years, keeping themselves apart from the suspicious Britons who remained in the area. The Anglo-saxons built family farmsteads scattered across the landscape, and the head of the family at upchester declared himself their chief.

Spindle Whorl

Spindle whorls were made from durable materials like clay, bone or stone. Small, and usually round or disc-shaped, with a hole in the middle, they provided weight and tension at the end of the thread when wool was spun.

Strands of fibre were teased out of a bundle of raw wool that had been put on a stick (the distaff), and were twisted into a thread and tied to the spindle. The whorl was fixed to the bottom of the spindle to weigh it down. The whorl and spindle were then twirled – twisting and teasing out more thread. This new thread was wound on to the spindle as it turned.

When all the wool had been spun it was woven into cloth.

urban excavations

Excavations in towns present a totally different set of problems to those on rural sites. A lot more challenging in many aspects, they can, equally, be more rewarding. Urban excavations are likely to include deep stratigraphy, layers upon layers of continuous occupation which have to be unravelled to understand what went on at the site. The first permanent towns began with the development of Roman settlements, such as York where occupation continued through the Saxon/Viking periods into the medieval and up to the present day. In other places occupation was interrupted – Cirencester, Gloucestershire, where the centre of the town shifted and the Roman town was sealed by large amounts of ploughsoil, is an example.

One of the biggest challenges with deeply stratified town sites is to identify different parts of the same layer when they have been cut through by later foundations, sewers and drains. This means that as the dig progresses, very detailed, precise records must be kept which identify the extent of each layer and, more importantly, its relationship to all other neighbouring layers.

soho in Birmingham with its industrial legacy, was a prime site for settlement analysis

Urban excavations are often located within plots of land which were laid out as tenements – long, narrow properties with street frontage and workshop behind – in the early life of the town and which still define modern ones as seen at the *Time Team* dig at Walmgate, York. It is preferable to dig the first trench from there to the back of the plot. This allows archaeologists to establish where the main building with its internal floor surfaces and hearths, and the outbuildings, yards and pits to the rear, will be situated. How buildings were constructed, together with finds from the site, help to indicate whether that part of the town was occupied by wealthy merchants and shopkeepers or was an area of craftsmen and individual activity.

A typical sequence of occupation may show that large amounts of hardcore were dumped on the ground to provide a firm foundation for a Saxon or early medieval timber building of which only a few post holes or beam slots survive.

Ship's Nails

Iron nails, usually heavily corroded, are often found on late medieval sites, and generally come from buildings – they were used to secure tiles to the roofs. 'Rove nails' or 'clench nails' fastened the timber boards of ships together and are less common but instantly recognizable. The ones pictured come from Smallhythe in Kent. They are much larger than domestic ones, about the size of an adult's middle finger, and were more like huge rivets than nails. A hole was bored where two timbers overlapped and a nail was posted through it, after which a 'rove' – a flat piece of iron like a washer, about 3 centimetres (1 inch) square with a hole in its centre – was placed over the pointed end of the nail. This protruded through the hole and was hammered flat so that it spread or folded over the rove and held the two timbers firmly together. Tarred wool was used to make the planks waterproof.

When ships and boats came to the end of their lives everything salvageable was removed and their hulls were left to rot away on the banks of waterways or on foreshores. Finding used rove nails on a site indicates the presence of one of these wrecks. The crucial piece of evidence for a site where ships were built rather than abandoned – the one *Time Team* excavated at Smallhythe, Kent, is an example – is a set of unused roves. These were made in strips divided up into squares, rather like a bar of chocolate, and were snapped off the strip one by one as needed. Finding one of these strips means that the roves were never used and strongly suggests that shipbuilding must have been carried out on or near a site.

As the town became more prosperous this structure, with its trampled earth floor and central hearth, might have been cut through by one with stone foundations. The imprint of this one would be defined in the ground by the foundation trenches. In some cases the stone foundations may survive, but all too frequently they have been robbed and the usable stone has been taken away for use elsewhere, so all that is left is a rubble-filled trench.

The remainder of the building can be reconstructed from architectural remains found in the demolition rubble. According to local tradition or fashion, the walls may have been stone, wattle and daub, or timber. Broken tiles or slates indicate the construction of the roof while fragments of window mouldings, glass or lead allow the windows to be reconstructed. A series of overlying floor surfaces of clay or fragments of floor tiles may be buried beneath the rubble. The demolition may have made way for the first brick structure on the site. Each episode of construction, demolition or alteration to the building is defined as a separate phase of activity.

Phil on... High Medieval Britain

I've dug deeply stratified urban medieval sites and found them very challenging and enjoyable, but more often than not excavations in Britain involve using a mechanical digger to strip off the topsoil down to the subsoil and then digging out the features. It's very much *Time Team* archaeology, as the constraint of three days means that trying to pick up details of the stratigraphy, and making sure they're fully recorded before you take off the next layer and go on down can't be done easily.

I remember that at Much Wenlock in Shropshire, way back in the mists of time, I had a little trench – a sondage – up against a boundary wall. We had put it in to discover the date of the wall. It was a lovely little trench. We got right to the bottom and found a piece of early medieval pottery, which proved that the boundary had been there for ages and ages. I felt really chuffed about that trench. Though it was mentioned in the programme, it wasn't covered in the detail I'd expected. That was a very important lesson for me because I'd spent three days down this hole and thought it was the bee's knees. I could have waxed lyrical about it, but point was that all it did was prove the date of the boundary, and televisually you can say that in one scene. The main thrust of the programme was what the standing buildings told us about how the medieval town of Much Wenlock had developed, but I was down that hole so I didn't see what good television they made.

One of the things I love is the woodworking techniques used in the roofs of medieval buildings. *Time Team* made a medieval roof truss for the cameo in the Plympton, Devon, programme and it was absolutely fascinating. I learnt so much about looking at timbers and loved listening to the people who were experts in the field. All the timbers in medieval structures were individually sawn and hewn, with the joints and pegs, and hoisted up by hand. It was an incredible achievement. You look at these old standing buildings and they're leaning, they bend, they bow, they buckle – they' re all over the place. Yet after about 500 years they're still there.

I haven't dug many castles but I remember one, Ludgershall Castle, where we mainly dug in the bailey, the wall round the outside. (The really nice bits in castles are the garderobe shafts – there are lots of interesting finds at the bottom of those!) However, I also had to draw the section through the drawbridge pit. We were a bit pushed for time at the end of the dig and the director of the excavation asked me whether I could draw a section. I was a fairly new digger and so I thought about post holes and things like that, about 15 centimetres (6 inches) deep, and said yes, I could draw a section. So he said, 'Draw that' – and there was this vast great drawbridge pit. It must have been about 4 metres (13 feet) deep. So I set up my horizontal string, as you do, and I put in the edges, top and bottom. That was easy enough. Then I sat down and put in a point here, and a point there, not really knowing which points on which layers I had to measure. I got more and more depressed. It seemed like I was there for an eternity. Eventually the director came back, asked how the section was going and looked at my drawing. He asked me to measure a few more points and then joined up the dots. I was astounded. Obviously I had known how to do the drawing – I just didn't have the confidence. I don't think I'll ever again be daunted by a section of that size.

settlement plan analysis

Settlement plan analysis is a method of finding out about the history and development of towns and villages where there is no early history or obvious archaeology, and involves looking at the patterns and alignments of boundaries, roads, tracks and lanes in the present landscape, and historical maps and documents. This type of work and approach was pioneered in towns (beginning with Alnwick in Northumberland and Ludlow, Shropshire) and has subsequently been used successfully in villages.

Some assessment of the sequence of development and the degree (or otherwise) of regularity is called for to make any sense of a town or village plan. There are usually pre-existing roads or boundaries whose alignment generally persists in any later developments. It is difficult to remove, divert or block roads, which are publicly used, without special powers. Different ownership of land on either side of a boundary usually preserves its alignment, although this can change if both sides come into one ownership.

It is usual for significant new areas of settlement to be added in cohesive blocks of properties that respect common boundaries and lanes. If the properties are planned there may be a regular pattern of rectangular ones, and even after hundreds of years this usually survives substantially intact (again because roads are common and different ownerships on either side of a boundary help to preserve it). Later developments can include subdividing or amalgamating properties, blocking roads or lanes, or cutting new roads across the earlier pattern, but it is seldom difficult to recognize that this has happened.

If a town or village is well documented it is possible to demonstrate clearly that a pattern of properties and local roads is, for example, of medieval or even earlier date. Excavations have shown how persistent many boundaries have been over hundreds of years.

Plan analysis therefore enables us to see something of the arrangement of earlier settlements even when nothing apparently survives from hundreds of years ago. How ironic that property boundaries and alignments of roads – rather than buildings, churches, castles and so on – should in the end prove to be the oldest and most enduring features of many places.

earthwork survey

On many archaeological sites the remains of walls, ditches, house platforms or defensive banks are visible as bumps and hollows in the ground, usually under grass pastures or even lawns. Earthwork survey, also commonly (but perhaps confusingly) known as field survey, involves recording and analyzing sites like these. It is much quicker than excavation, but slower than aerial photography. And while it provides less information than digging, it records a lot more than is visible on a photograph taken from the air.

Earthworks can survive almost anywhere that the ground has been undisturbed or a building has lain for any length of time, but some of the most common sites are deserted medieval villages, such as High Worsall in Yorkshire – the subject of a *Time Team* investigation in 1998. Here, the village street is visible as a long hollow where countless feet tramping backwards and forwards had worn away the ground surface, while the house sites can be seen as platforms raised above the street. In many cases the walls of the houses are low banks on top of the platforms, while the boundaries that had divided one plot from its neighbour can be seen running at right angles to the street.

High Worsall from the air, showing the earthworks of the village and the medieval ridge and furrow in the field to the right

Sites like this must be accurately planned and carefully interpreted if they are to be understood properly, so it is necessary to record the exact position and size of all the 'lumps and bumps' on a plan. This is done by using either a global positioning by satellite (GPS) system, or by measuring a series of 'control' points, usually with a 'total stations' electronic theodolite and distance measurer (EDM). This is set up on one of the control points and measures, quickly and accurately, the distance between, and direction of, all the other points in view. On a small site the control can be as simple as two points, one at either end of the earthworks. On larger, more complex sites there may be tens, or even hundreds, of them.

A simple version of this technique is to use a straight base-line or set up a grid control with a right-angled triangle – one with sides in the ratio 3:4:5. The distances to roads or the corners of fields are measured and the control points that result are fitted into an Ordnance Survey map. One tape measure is laid out between them and another is offset at right angles to measure the distances between the tops and bottoms of slopes. These are marked on the site plan. Archaeologists use symbols or 'hachures' of different lengths to indicate slopes in the ground. Each one looks like a 'Y' with the top filled in and a line of these is used to depict each slope: the solid ends are at the top and the thin ones at the bottom.

The real skill in earthwork survey is in working out exactly what features are on a site, and how they relate to one another. It is not always easy to spot the less obvious slopes and surveyors often have to 'squat and squint' to see exactly what is going on. It is also crucial to identify which features overlie or cut through others so that archaeologists can establish their chronological order: if a ditch cuts through a bank, the bank must be earlier than the ditch. At High Worsall, the earthwork survey suggested, firstly, that because all the properties were the same size the village had been laid out in two planned blocks. And secondly, that because the earthworks in one of them were less obvious than in the other it had been the first to be abandoned. Thirdly, the survey suggested that a central part of the settlement had been occupied before either of the two planned blocks were built and that it had been more haphazardly laid out. All of which was proved to be correct by *Time Team's* excavations.

Medieval Pottery

Although medieval pottery is found in large quantities, it is not as abundant as either Roman or post-medieval wares (1450–1750), nor is it of such good quality. It includes bowls, jugs and cooking pots and is generally earthenware, made from local clay tempered with sand, crushed stone, grit or shell. Fired in specially constructed kilns, earthenware pots are fired at below 1,000°C, rather than over 1,100°C used for stonewares. The rim and base forms of the pots vary, which enables archaeologists to date and source the wares. Rims can be either inverted or upright, and these can be rolled rim or grooved lip, or flat top with a rolled rim, or almost any variation of these styles. The forms are probably fairly localized.

From the fourteenth century, the industry seemed to pick up. More regional potteries were established and decoration became more elaborate. Pots began to be painted with designs of varying colours and figures of animals or humans. Lead glazes were commonly used, giving the pots a green, yellow or brown colour. This was not the first time glazes have been used – some pots in the late Saxon period were glazed – but it was on a greater scale than before. Glazing improved the quality of the medieval pots, making the surfaces impervious. However, the standard cooking pot was still unglazed and purely functional, but by the late medieval period, ornamented pottery was widespread.

Mick on... High Medieval sites

monk, because that is what studious chaps did, but I wouldn't have been very happy about it.

The best kind of find from the early Middle Ages would be something personal like a pair of shoes that would bring the people of the time close, like the ones we found at Walmgate in York – and it would have to be waterlogged in order to have survived the centuries. I wouldn't want a sword or armour because loads of swords have been found and most people, for most of their lives, had nothing to do with warfare.

The wonderful thing about the medieval period is that there are incredibly useful documents that help to explain the archaeology. The most useful for studying a town like Timechester would be the rental record for 1200 or 1300 as it would list all the properties, the owners and their occupations, and the size of the plots. This is the best kind of information to have when you are excavating this kind of site. The *Domesday Book* is another good source to refer to. It dates to 1086 and would have recorded Timechester in great detail – not many places were missed out of the survey.

Similar medieval and post-medieval records are available for towns or properties that were owned by one individual who kept records of his estate. In the same way, the only reason we know about Stratford-upon-Avon is because its bishop recorded all properties, their rentals and the names and trades of the people who lived in them. The names are interesting because the record was made when Stratford was only one generation old. At the time, people took their surnames from the place where they were born so it is possible to trace their origins. The names listed in the record show that 70 per cent of the people came from within 9.5 kilometres (6 miles) of Stratford. They had presumably come there and decided to stay. You can actually see the town taking off.

Plympton in Devon is an offshoot of Plymouth and was a thriving medieval village in the twelfth and thirteenth centuries. It was a planned settlement based around a motte and bailey castle. *Time Team* rooted around in the cellars, gardens and lofts of people's houses and discovered that a lot more building features had survived from the Middle Ages than was previously thought. Like Plympton, much of the medieval town would survive today in Timechester's buildings.

The landscape around modern Timechester, like the countryside surrounding other towns, shows more traces from the Middle Ages than from any other period. In fact, although enclosure – converting common land into private property from the fifteenth and sixteenth centuries onwards – produced the modern English landscape, and many of its features have earlier antecedents, it is impossible to understand what we see today without referring to the medieval pattern of settlements, agriculture and strip fields. Field systems, in particular, are important: I reckon that in two-thirds of England the patterns we see now are based on what would have been there in the Middle Ages. Tracks, roads and lanes also relate to the medieval landscape.

I wouldn't have liked living in the Middle Ages. If I had had to live then I would have been a

CHAPTER 8
post-medieval

carenza's story of Timechester in 1645

Nearly 400 years have passed since 1250, and Timechester in 1645 is both familiar and changed. The main street still runs along the same route, and many of the houses occupy the same spots although they are now much taller. The stone walls of the town, built in 1240, are now old: the gates at either end of the street still stand where the Roman gates stood, but they are in need of repair and are crumbling under military attack. The church, too, is still in the same place, but it looks very different with graceful arches and a tall steeple. The castle has also changed: the solid square keep has gone and is replaced by a more ornate but less defendable range of stone and brick buildings built around a circular courtyard which was once the castle mound. Outside the town walls ramshackle buildings along Northgate Street are more solidly built but are still smaller than those inside them. Small boats ply their way up and down the Time River, while hulks of larger boats lie rotting on its banks. Perhaps most startlingly, the village of Sutton has disappeared: just a few bumps in the ground mark its former site. But the area is not totally deserted – nearby stands a large mansion surrounded by a moat and ornate geometrically laid-out gardens, all in glorious isolation within a large park which has incorporated much of the earlier village's field system. Elsewhere the fields are still a swathe of corrugated ridges, but downriver from Timechester some of the larger fields have now been divided up into smaller, squarer, hedged units within which the older curving ridges are still clearly visible. What is the story behind these four centuries of continuity and change in Timechester?

The wall the townspeople and lord of Timechester started around 1230 gave them great satisfaction but, even when it was first built, it only enclosed the centre of the town: it was for prestige rather than defence of the community and defined, simply but effectively, the limit of the zone of higher-status plots which came with privileges that included lower taxes. Most of the occupants of the houses on these plots were traders but other people were also attracted to Timechester and occupied the cheaper plots just outside the city walls. Making pottery, fulling cloth or tanning hides were dirty, smelly activities that were not welcomed within the town itself, and as occupations they were not as respectable as being a merchant. Neither were they as profitable as trade, but a hardworking or talented individual could support his family by making a decent living from any of them, free from the burdens of life on the rural manor of Sutton where a tenth of the crops a peasant produced had to go to the parish priest and at least one day a week had to be spent working for the lord. A peasant who left the manor would incur severe punishment if he were caught and returned, but it was relatively easy to vanish anonymously into the bustle of Timechester where he would be able to find work and set up home. Ideally this would be as close to the city walls as possible, and many houses and small

industries sprang up alongside the two roads leading into the town at Northgate and Southgate.

As in the eighth century, Timechester's location was in its favour. Pottery and leather goods were traded in its market but it was the export of wool, much of it destined for the Europe where it was made into cloth, that enabled many merchants to make their fortunes. As their wealth increased they enlarged their

A jettied building in Much Wenlock

houses, but there were soon no vacant plots left in the town centre and by 1300 the few spaces between houses on the prestigious main street and marketplace had long been sold off or given to sons or daughters. This resulted in increasingly narrow plots facing on to the streets and the only way to make the houses bigger was by making them higher, with upper floors that jutted over the street to create the largest possible amount of living space.

Although the lord no longer received rents and tolls from houses and trade in the town, the castle remained his home, supported by revenue from his large rural estates. Like the merchants, he too wanted his residence to reflect his wealth and status as a powerful lord, but he also wanted it to be comfortable enough to accommodate guests – even the king. The castle therefore had to look strong, but also opulent and ostentatiously expensive, built in the latest style. Work finally began around 1290, after much thought. He had the square Norman keep replaced by a circular courtyard building while the bailey was rebuilt as a stone curtain wall, with stables, kitchens and accommodation for his retinue, including men-at-arms and domestic servants, arranged alongside its inner side.

The wealth of the lord and the merchants was not spent only on their houses. Mindful of the need to ensure their well-being in the next world as well as that of medieval Timechester, they also gave money to the Church. this had paid for a major rebuilding of St Mary's in the late thirteenth century when a magnificent new building replaced the earlier structure with its amalgam of Saxon and Norman architectural styles.

But the good times did not continue unchecked. In the decade after 1310 three failed harvests and outbreaks of disease among sheep and cattle herds pushed up food prices in Timechester – and caused even greater hardship in Sutton where it was difficult to find alternative sources of food. Despite the penalties, men and women occasionally left the manor for nearby towns and the population of the village began to dip. But worse was to come. In 1348 a particularly virulent outbreak of plague, dubbed the Black Death, was in full spate, and was soon brought to Timechester by travelling tradesmen. The disease spread rapidly through the densely packed town and more than a third of the population died in just over eighteen months. For a while the streets and marketplace were quieter than they had been for 500 years. The countryside was nearly as badly affected. Of the sixty or so adults aged over fourteen who were living in Sutton in 1345 only thirty-eight were left by 1349. Four parish priests died in a single year as each replacement succumbed to the dreaded disease, which he caught while ministering to the dying.

By the end of 1349 the Black Death had run its course but in the Time Valley, as in most of England, the aftermath lasted for many years. The survivors still had to eat, but there were few people left in the country to produce food. Rural lords, desperate for manual labour, would pay good wages with few questions asked and made no attempt to return renegade peasants to the manor of their birth. Within ten years of the outbreak of the plague six families had left Sutton, some for other rural manors, others for Timechester where, for the first time in living memory, vacant plots were available at low rents.

Even the town was slow to recover. At the beginning of the fifteenth century, in an attempt to restore prosperity, one family after another turned to the production of cloth: this added considerably to the value of the wool that had been a feature of the Timechester region for so long, and resulted in greater profits. Shipbuilding also took place on the banks of the Time and industry began to grow in Timechester.

Sutton was not so lucky. The lord realized too late that he should release his peasants from their feudal duties and obligations and pay them fairer wages for their labour if he wanted them to stay – Timechester attracted people away from the increasingly hard life in the shrinking village. By 1428

there were only nine households left in Sutton, so pathetically few that they were exempted from national taxes in an attempt to save the settlement. But a few decades later things reached crisis point: there were not even enough people to keep all the fields in production – sowing, weeding and reaping them was beyond the capacity of the four families that now remained. At a meeting of the manorial court the lord announced his solution: most of the land, including the largely deserted village, would be turned over to sheep pasture for wool production which required few workers and seemed to be profitable. He could pay a few villagers to farm his own land, but they would no longer be allowed to farm any themselves. Just two families stayed on, living in new tied cottages far away from the village that had been home to their ancestors for 700 years.

The gamble paid off for the lord. Wool from sheep grazing on the former strip fields did indeed produce a good profit, and within a generation his family had rebuilt Sutton manor house and surrounded it with gardens laid out in fashionable geometric patterns, all within a massive park in which deer were kept for hunting: a convenient supply of fresh meat. The remains of the abondoned peasant houses were cleared away, to improve the view.

Far from London, long the undisputed capital of England and by far its largest town, the Time Valley was rarely involved in national events. But in 1588 it came close to one when a ship was wrecked off the coast near Timechester. The vessel had been part of the Armada Philip II of Spain had assembled to invade England. Defeated by a combination of English tactics and the weather, the surviving ships had tried to escape, but by no means all of them made it back to Spain – the Timechester wreck was one of the many unlucky ones. The spoil that washed ashore, including a chest of Spanish gold, gave rise to many gleeful celebrations in Timechester.

The town's shipbuilding industry did not have a chance to gloat, however. By 1600 it was a thing of the past, doomed by the gradual silting up of the river which made it impassable for the larger ships that were being built elsewhere. But Timechester survived the loss and by 1640 it was again reasonably prosperous and expanding. Although the town walls were no longer regularly maintained the area within them was once more packed with houses, in plots which were increasingly subdivided, and beyond the walls the suburbs were spreading. There seemed to be little need for strong defences – until civil war broke out in 1642.

Following the example of the lord in his castle, the people of Timechester supported Charles I and at first it seemed that they had backed the winner. But the tide soon turned against the Royalists, and in 1645 the town was attacked by Parliamentarian troops. The lord was away fighting for the king, but for six days his wife and household defended the castle successfully against volleys of cannonballs. Eventually, however, the walls of the castle, which were not really built for defence, gave way to a particularly sustained attack. As the Roundheads poured in many of the defenders died in a hail of musket fire, and the lady of the castle and her children were taken prisoner.

underwater archaeology

It is strange that a nation as steeped in naval history as Britain should do so little about caring for its nautical archaeology. It is estimated that there are between 150,000 and 250,000 wrecked ships around its coastline and of these only 35,000 are known and only fifty are registered as protected – these include the late sixteenth-century wreck off Teignmouth in south Devon which *Time Team* examined. Fortunately, people are increasingly aware of the information that can be recovered from wrecks and divers are becoming more conscientious about reporting ones that appear to have potential archaeological interest.

final equipment checks before going underwater at Finlaggan

Equipment is the first priority when excavating under water and it is essential to check this and air supplies before starting – apart from anything else, diving has to be carefully controlled as changes in pressure affect the human body, which means that there are no opportunities to return to the site hut to collect forgotten pieces of equipment. The digging process itself is similar to that on land, although churning up the silt on the seabed means that visibility may be greatly reduced. Spoken communication is impossible under water and excavators need to work together via sign language and natural cooperation.

Excavated spoil is removed by an air lift, which is like a giant vacuum cleaner. It quickly draws the fine silt up through a tube and dumps it on the seabed downcurrent of the site, leaving heavier objects. In some ways, this makes finds more visible, almost like wet-sieving on land. Site notes, plans and sections are made directly on waterproof film and the information is transferred to the main site record. Layers of sediment are treated in exactly the same as they would be on land – excavators even use trowels to remove them.

Although many wrecks are the remains of abandoned vessels that were left on shores, most are the result of catastrophic events at sea and carry powerful stories like the battle with the Spanish Armada and the seventeenth- and eighteenth-century slave trade. Each one represents a time capsule that was sealed when it sank. If seabed deposits formed rapidly on a ship, making its structure impervious to water, organic remains, the like of which are rarely found on land, can be preserved, like shoes, bodies and timbers. Excavating, recording and lifting these can be time consuming. Once on shore they must be treated immediately to prevent them drying out and decomposing. They are stored in a similar environment to that in which they were found, usually sea water, and the salt in the water is gradually reduced and washed out of the timbers. They are then conserved by a specialist.

Seventeenth-Century Slipwares

Pottery decorated with slips, or liquid clay, of various colours and made in country potteries such as Verwood in Dorset and Donyatt in Somerset, was popular during the seventeenth and early eighteenth centuries, and remained in use until the nineteenth. These are seventeenth-century examples from Stoke-on-Trent, dated by the patterns on their surfaces.

The colour of the slip often contrasted with that of the clay from which the pottery was made. For example, a thin orange-brown layer would be applied over a red pot. Yellow lines and patterns, or decorations like pictures, lettering and dates, were sometimes added and the whole surface was then glazed. Variations included sgraffito ware, where lines were scratched through the slip to show the colour beneath, and feathered patterns which were achieved by dragging a bristle through the liquid clay.

architectural survey

Many structures from the Middle Ages and earlier have survived above ground in standing buildings, which have often been altered over the centuries to keep up to date with the latest fashions, rather than being demolished. Changes in construction methods, materials and architectural style mean that different parts of a building, from different periods, can be dated quite accurately.

At Plympton, Devon, many houses on the main street appear to be Georgian, but when *Time Team* investigated it became clear that they were much older and that their frontages had been redesigned in the eighteenth century. Vital clues can be found in areas like attics. Medieval roof timbers are identified by their characteristic curving shapes or distinctive tooling on their under surfaces. If they are blackened by soot it suggests that the house started life as a medieval hall, which would have been open from the ground to the roof with no floors in between.

Crucial clues are also often found in cellar beams or details around windows, doorways or fireplaces. However, caution is needed in dating an entire building from features such as these as they may been have salvaged from other buildings and reused. If this has happened these architectural clues will be older than the building.

The shape and size of the bricks and other materials used in walls can be highly significant. Tudor bricks, for example, are much flatter than those used in later buildings, which enabled *Time Team* to date different parts of the buildings at Rycote in Oxfordshire. If the walls are made of stone the style of workmanship can be crucial: Saxon tooling is distinctively different from later medieval work, for example, and this helped us to date stone at Thetford Priory in Norfolk. Late medieval stone blocks often have strange chiselled marks made by masons who were paid to shape them on a piecework basis and wanted to be sure they received payment for everything they produced. *Time Team* found marks by two different masons in the hall at Aston Eyre, Shropshire.

In many old buildings every wall will have a tale to tell, although the evidence is often hidden underneath layers of plaster or rendering. There was no render on the back wall at Aston Eyre shown here so all the details were plain to see – blocked-in doorways, rebuilt windows and truncated walls that had once formed part of another room but had been levelled flat when that part of the building was demolished. At Bawsey, Norfolk, an observant eye could detect a similarly detailed history of alteration, enhancement and improvement in the church wall. Buildings like these can be recorded as three-dimensional plans similar to those of modern architects. Particularly complex walls need to be recorded as carefully as a trench: every stone, brick or timber must be measured and drawn to scale. Using electronic surveying techniques and software, it is now possible to record a wall by marking several points on it, taking a photograph and then fitting the points on this over the points on the plan to eliminate distortion – if this was not done, anything away from the very centre of the photograph would be in slightly the wrong place. Not a problem with holiday snaps, but a serious handicap if straight walls are recorded as slanted or bending! A detailed plan is then drawn and the succession of phases of alteration is teased out.

It is a sobering thought that an intricate succession of rebuilding and alteration revealed by an architectural survey will often leave no trace in the foundations – which are all that archaeologists normally have to work with.

surveying a building at aston eyre, old windows and roofs can clearly be seen

Phil on... Post-medieval Britain

What lodges in my mind about Basing House in Hampshire is not so much the excavation itself but the story that it told. There's something very powerful about the disasters *Time Team* has investigated: the plane crashes at Reedham Marshes in Norfolk and Wierre-Effroy in northern France, the shipwreck at Teignmouth in Devon – and the fall of Basing House during the Civil War. They are specifically recorded events so you know exactly when they happened and there's a very personal aspect. For the poor devils holed up in Basing House it must have been a very, very frightening experience, with Parliamentarians coming through, the building falling down around their ears, gunpowder exploding. When you're digging and reach that burnt layer, you think, 'My God, people were dying here. People were killing one another.' It's strange to think of those Royalists holed up in a burning building, knowing that if they poked their heads out of a window somebody would shoot them. I'd hate to be in that predicament – I'm sure I'd panic. It's the power of the story that I remember about Basing House.

One of the nice things is to test written records against actual finds and at Basing the question was whether we could find any physical evidence of the battle described in documents. We could. There were burnt levels, and musket balls with flat surfaces where they had impacted on walls and armour. All right, we didn't find bits of arms and legs and weaponry, but those musket balls weren't from a pheasant shoot! I remember Robin Bush, *Time Team*'s history expert, saying that the Parliamentarians melted down the lead coffins of Royalists and used the metal to make the balls. Basing was well documented and we knew the style of architecture, so though the house wasn't actually standing, we had a fair idea of what it would have looked like.

It's not always as easy as that. At Basing we were also looking for another house – a Stuart mansion built after Basing House itself. We did find it, but it was difficult working out which bit we found. The plan we had was a very stylized representation of the house that had been there. Also the scale on the plan was so small that it was difficult to plot the foundations precisely. To me, the plan just said that there was a building of a particular style on this spot – and, through our excavation, we showed that it was there.

Standing-building archaeology is a science in its own right. A lot of the really interesting detail is often covered by render or plaster, so when this is removed you've got the entire history of the building without actually having to put a spade in the ground. The things to look for are different styles of brick-bonding, different mortars, blocked-up windows and new doorways. You also need to look in the backfill of the wall foundations to establish when the building was put up – and probably at the floors to see when it was in use. In a number of cases there are no wall foundations, just robbed-out trenches filled with rubble, and you look at these for clues to when the structure was dismantled – at the palace in Richmond, Surrey, the remains of a seventeenth-century bellarmine jug in a trench that had been robbed out told us when the building had been knocked down.

Musket Balls

The development of firearms like pistols and muskets in the sixteenth and seventeenth centuries resulted in a whole technology of gunpowder and ammunition production, and a new vocabulary that is still in use – 'flash in the pan', for example, and 'keep your powder dry'.

Small lead balls were used as ammunition. They varied in size according to the bore of the firearm and were cast in a mould that consisted of two halves – the join can often by seen in surviving examples. The successors of flint arrowheads and the predecessors of modern bullets, musket balls could inflict considerable damage and there are examples of armour that has been dented by them. The armour Victor is holding here has been pierced by a musket ball. Balls that are flattened as result of hitting structures like walls have also been found.

Window Glass and Cames

In medieval and Saxon times glass was expensive to produce and using it in windows was a luxury enjoyed only by the Church, and by the wealthiest families – who removed their glass from its frames and took it with them when they visited their various manors.

During the Roman period cross-shaped metal retainers were used to fix square panes of glass into wooden frames, but a different method was employed during the Middle Ages. Pieces of glass, often of varying shapes and sizes, were held in place by strips of lead called cames which were H-shaped in section to hold the glass and were cut to length and heated until they were pliable enough to be joined together. A selection of glass and came pieces can be seen above, from the site of Basing House. Complex patterns could be built up especially if, as was often the case, the glass was painted or stained. The window was then fixed into a frame and held in place by metal glazing bars.

Mick on... Post-medieval sites

Towns took years to recover from the Black Death which devastated Britain in the middle of the fourteenth century, and it was the sixteenth century before they resumed business as usual. So what most people think of as being medieval towns, with gable-ended roofs and buildings with upper floors that jut over the street, are in fact post-medieval and date from the sixteenth and seventeenth centuries. Most of York is from that period, and *Time Team*'s finds at Plympton in Devon were typical of the kind of post-medieval evidence that survives in towns. However, there can' t be many towns in Britain where late-medieval roofs, wall plaster and vaults under pavements haven't been found. Unfortunately, the whole exercise of cataloguing historic buildings went wrong because most of them were listed according to their outside appearance, whereas most of the medieval structure is hidden inside.

In the late sixteenth century Timechester, like other towns in Britain, had its prestigious residences, reflecting a trend that was linked with the redistribution of land – a development that was crucial in shaping the landscape of the post-medieval period. When Henry VIII dissolved the English and Welsh monasteries between 1536 and 1539 some 20 per cent of their lands went to the crown. During the next ten years the king granted these to his followers and people all over Britain acquired new estates.

Each landowner then needed a decent country house and, although some of them revamped medieval buildings, new styles were introduced. In particular, the use of differently shaped and sized bricks became popular, especially in eastern parts of the country. Wealthy merchants lived in towns, cheek by jowl with labourers, at this time. However, in about the eighteenth century it became fashionable to live in the country and they built country houses for themselves, and surrounded the mansions with parks.

In the sixteenth century, anyone who came into a fortune or made money through land distribution displayed their wealth by buying Venetian glass and Spanish pottery, and hoped for the ultimate status symbol: a visit from Henry VIII or, later, Elizabeth I. Not only could this result in further lucrative positions for the host, it would also demonstrate his newly aquired status. However, having the monarch as a guest was a double-edged sword because more often than not the visit resulted in bankruptcy.

The best example of this was at a site I was involved in studying at Iron Acton, near Bristol, where a beautiful house was built, a medieval moat was filled in because it was out of fashion and many high-status pieces of glass and pottery were brought in. Henry VIII descended on the house for a week and bankrupted the family – who unfortunately got nothing from him in return. In excavation, the house and everything we found in it only made sense because we knew of this one visit from documentary evidence. The tree-ring date for all the timbers in the building is exactly a year before the king came to Iron Acton, proving that the house was purpose-built for him. All the glass and pottery seems to have been smashed during the visit. It must have been a hell of a party.

CHAPTER 9
early modern

carenza's story of timechester in 1800

J ust 150 years have passed since the English Civil War but even in this short time Timechester has seen profound changes. Most noticeably, in 1800 it is much larger than ever before. New streets with houses packed together have mushroomed, spreading over former farmland on all sides of the town. Equally dramatically, the castle has vanished and in its place there is an elegant curving crescent of fine new houses. The town walls have almost disappeared: just a few traces survive on either side of the gates, which are mostly intact though in poor repair. However, the line of the walls can be traced in the pattern of the streets that run alongside the walls. St Mary's church has fared better – new aisles have been added and the nave has been raised by the addition of a clerestorey. The main street still follows its long-established course, but looks very different. Most of the old timber-framed houses have been replaced by an elegant row of square stone buildings – but in many cases the change is only skin-deep as the houses behind the facades retain much of their medieval character. The imposing town hall that faces on to the marketplace is new. Many of the long building plots which previously contained orchards or elegant gardens now contain workshops. Other, larger, buildings have also appeared since 1645, most notably the vast factory in the grounds of Sutton Manor and the huge bottle-shaped edifices by the river. Also near the river, there is a new waterway – a canal, host to several heavily loaded barges. Also new is the elegant monument on Timebury Hill within the ancient hillfort. How has Timechester managed to change so much in such a short period of time?

The siege of 1645 was a disaster for the last lord of Timechester. His wife and children were only released on the payment of a heavy fine and the castle itself was ransacked and left uninhabitable – the family would not have cared to live there even if they had been given the choice. But they were not: the buildings and land were

confiscated by Parliament. Everything of value, down to the lead from the roof and even the very walls themselves, was sold off. By 1670 the site lay derelict for the first time in nearly 1,000 years.

Much of Timechester was also damaged in the siege. Like the castle, it was ransacked because it was a Royalist stronghold and many houses were burnt down, especially in the suburbs outside its walls. But unlike the castle the town recovered: it was in no one's interest, townspeople or Parliament, for it to be

permanently destroyed. Houses were rebuilt on their previous sites – they occupied exactly the same spaces but were now constructed of stone rather than timber and wattle – while the processing of locally produced wool into finished cloth continued to prove lucrative. The problem of the river silting up did not, as some had expected, sound Timechester's death knell. Although the shipbuilding industry never recovered, the town's position as a centre of trade and commerce continued. This was largely due to the entrepreneurial acumen of one family, the Tinneys, who,

in 1670, were granted a royal charter to set up a new settlement on their land at the mouth of the Time River. Timemouth was an immediate success. Within fifty years its harbour was receiving a constant stream of ships that loaded and unloaded a rapidly increasing range of goods – cloth was exported to Europe, while there was money to be made in Britain by trading goods such as tobacco from the New World. Merchandise from the ships was ferried or driven the five miles upriver to Timechester's ancient market. Timemouth's carefully laid-out gridded streets soon housed 2,000 people, while the population of Timechester grew in both size and wealth on the profits of international trade: by the early years of the

eighteenth century the Tinney family was making its fortune from its sugar plantation in the Carribbean.

In the early 1700s pressure on space within Timechester began to rise again. Most of the building plots of the medieval town had been subdivided to a quarter of their original width and it had long been impossible to erect new buildings that faced on to the main street, but good money could be made by renting out workshops at the back of the long plots. Narrow lanes up the sides of the plots linked them to the main streets of the rapidly growing town. Despite the demand for building land, the oval site of the castle remained a largely empty communal space, used occasionally for fairs and public entertainment. But in about 1740 one John Trantor used profits made from trading slaves to acquire the empty

one of the georgian town houses in the centre of plympton

land on the castle site for building. But he did not use it to rehouse the cramped occupants in the building plots: instead he commissioned a terrace of elegant houses in the latest classical style, planned in a sweeping circle around the oval castle site. They were expensive, fashionable residences for those who were making their fortunes in the flourishing town and who wanted new, stylish homes with elegant, light, airy reception rooms where visitors could be entertained in style and treated to the latest fashionable delicacy – hot coffee and chocolate, served in tiny porcelain cups. Everyone knew that both cups and contents had to be imported at huge expense from opposite ends of the earth, so there was no better way for someone to show off their position in society. In this period of exciting newness, no one was interested in looking after the town walls and they crumbled away as their stone was pillaged for building; only the towers on either side of the old town gates were occasionally repaired if one too many blows from passing carts made them unstable.

In the countryside the past was more enduring. Folk memories of the depopulation of Sutton were still vivid and the the lord who finally turned the settlement over to sheep and deer had been demonized as a merciless and greedy destroyer. In the late seventeenth century the owners of Sutton Manor returned much of their land to arable farming, hoping to profit from supplying grain to the growing population of Timechester. But this proved to be a bad mistake: the family lost huge sums of money because of wrongly anticipating flutuating grain prices and the great house and gardens became an expensive burden.

In eighteenth-century Timechester, two new enterprises further stimulated the town's economy. Joseph Spodewood's family had been potters for generations, but in about 1760 Joseph leased a new site just outside the town near the river. Making use of the plentiful local clay and coal, he established a pottery manufacturing site and constructed a series of huge bottle-shaped brick-built kilns, each of which could fire thousands of objects. His obsession with experimenting with new techniques of glazing and firing soon paid off. Within a few years his attractive cream-coloured Spodewood cups, plates, jugs and dishes occupied pride of place on tables across Britain. But travel by road was slow and expensive, and Joseph was quick to see the potential benefits of a canal, which would allow rapid and cheap transportation of his products. He campaigned hard for such a waterway and he was a man who usually got what he wanted. By 1800 a canal linked Timechester with Timemouth and many other inland towns and cities. Although Joseph was a superb businessman, he was also generous, with a strong community spirit, and by 1790 he was making plans to raise money to build a new town hall on one side of the marketplace.

Just ten years after Spodewood had set up his works, Matthias Moulton established a very different manufacturing site on the other side of the River Time. He designed a huge brick-built range of buildings to house a giant complex of machinery powered by the steam engines he had invented. Moulton's factory was soon pouring out tens of thousands of coins for use in the New World, along with buttons, buckles and trinkets – all mass-produced more quickly and more cheaply than had ever been possible before. Moulton was soon able to purchase Sutton Manor from the poverty-stricken family who had been there since the Norman conquest. He demolished the house and rebuilt it as a grand mansion in the latest Palladian style. The fussy and hopelessly old-fashioned geometric gardens were swept away and replaced by open vistas of lakes and trees – all newly created and planted. Moulton was particularly pleased with his elegant stone monument on Timebury Hill from where he could admire his lands and the growing town of Timechester.

canals provided cheaper and more efficient transport in the late seventeenth century

The countryside was also adapting to new ways. The land between Timechester and the sea was increasingly taken over by expanding settlement, while the remaining agricultural land was also reorganized. The old curving ridges of the communal medieval strip-field prairies were overlain by private rectangular fields hedged with hawthorn as government policies encouraged landowners to maximize their yields. A new farm, called Canada Farm after the country where its owner had made his fortune, was built in the middle of this newly rearranged farmland. It was laid out in accordance with the new principles of farming, which stipulated the layout of the buildings around a courtyard down to the tiniest detail, even determining the position of the manure sheds.

By 1800 Timechester was three times the size it had been in 1645. The new factories were noisy and dirty, while suburbs were extending in every direction, almost engulfing the factories and overrunning land that had been arable for centuries. A few families had become very wealthy but the number of very poor people, crowded into increasingly inadequate housing, was growing worryingly fast.

industrial archeology

On many of the sites from this period, the upper industrial layers are simply machined off. They are regarded as a modern disturbance, contamination of the true archaeology. However, industrial archaeology has become a study in its own right and the investigation of recent industrial activities is widespread across Britain. Sites such as the Ironbridge Gorge and the Cornish tin mines are well studied and have become popular visitor centres.

phil excavating a petrol tank at soho, just one of the many problems that can be encountered on an industrial site

The differences in stratigraphy are much clearer on industrial or recent sites than they are on older ones, probably because they have not undergone similar soil formation processes. For example, a fall of bricks will form a very clear layer in the archaeology of an industrial site. However, on a prehistoric one a feature like a ditch will be affected by disturbances that have occurred over thousands of years: earthworms will have mixed the earth, roots will have pushed into the layers, clay will have been washed down through the soil. All this results in the stratigraphy becoming blurred. With industrial archaeology, it is more black and white.

Excavating industrial sites is not without its problems. The sheer nature of the processes involved in modern industry causes severe problems with chemical contamination and the scale of manufacturing is such that the quantity of waste is magnified many times. An example is the recent *Time Team* excavation at Blaenavon in south Wales. Here the whole landscape was totally artificial: hills and valleys had been altered and created and there was an enormous amount of waste material. The industrial waste itself was not actually contaminated, but the 1970s refuse that lay on top of it was unsavoury. This obviously created a number of potential safety hazards which had to be dealt with.

In many cases these hazards can be anticipated before the start of an excavation. It is someone's responsibility to find out whether there will be any contaminated areas or dangerous substances on site, where they are and what repercussions they will have on the health and safety of the excavators. Protective clothing is often required and special experts are consulted. At Reedham Marshes in Norfolk, spilt aviation fuel was highly corrosive to unprotected hands, and an RAF bomb-disposal team was needed to deal with the live ammunition that still littered the site where a bomber had crashed.

The risk of contamination is higher on urban sites than rural ones because they have been developed more extensively. Service pipes and modern intrusions will affect an excavation and preparation is necessary to identify the problem areas. Although features such as gas mains, sewers, electric cables or petrol tanks should be acccurately marked on local council plans this is not always the case and occasionally an unexpected water pipe is hit and needs patching, or a petrol tank is discovered and has to be made safe, as happened during *Time Team*'s excavation at Soho in Birmingham.

Blue and White Wares

Blue and white pottery – white inside with a white glaze and blue decoration on the outside – is one of the most common finds in gardens throughout Britain and also on archaeological sites from this period. It is still made, of course, but its origins go back to at least the seventeenth century.

People were immensely impressed with the beautifully decorated – and expensive – Chinese porcelain that came to western Europe in the late sixteenth century and there were many attempts to copy it. This was achieved in the seventeenth century in Delft, in Holland, where potters produced glazed earthenware hand-painted in blue on a white background, and from the early eighteenth century this delftware was widely made in England. Its success depended on using better quality clays including, from the eighteenth century, Cornish china clay (kaolin) tempered with crushed flint or ground-up bone. With the development of transfer printing – the use of prepared designs rather than ones painted on by hand – highly decorated pottery became generally affordable and masses of blue and white wares were produced.

typological dating

Before the development of absolute dating methods like dendrochronology and radiocarbon dating, archaeologists had to rely on typological dating to give them an idea of what period a site came from. Typological dating is achieved by comparing artefacts of the same type, and deciding which one comes first and which comes later. The site or layer with the earlier style is therefore older than the site or layer with the more recent style.

The decision about which is older is usually based on the theory that artefact styles change over time, and so the simpler artefact is older than the more complex. From this you can build up a sequence of styles from the oldest to the most recent. For example you can look at prehistoric axes. The stone ones are the earliest because they are just shaped from a piece of stone. Later came copper and bronze axes for which you had to extract and manipulate the metal, and then shape it. Even within

Phil on... Early Modern Britain

I'm very fond of industrial archaeology – it's good stuff. What I associate most with the period that produced it is dark satanic mills. They were very dark and satanic then, but now that a lot of them are being done up and made into exclusive apartments you can see that they were attractive buildings in their own right. And I love the steam industry – it's very much like a snorting, raging bull with people shovelling on coal, and great big pulleys and pistons, and thundering machines. It was a very vibrant technology, with lots of action, and it created our modern world.

I have never seen as much pottery as there was at the Burslem excavation in Stoke-on-Trent. There was so much I was overwhelmed by it, almost helpless. That's not to say I didn't love it. Industrial archaeology has the potential to create larger amounts of material than almost any other type – and this doesn't necessarily apply only to the eighteenth and nineteenth centuries. If you look at the industrial archaeology of the Neolithic period, it created a hell of a lot of spoil, and with no mechanization at all. At Blaenavon in south Wales all the ironworking and tinworking was done by hand.

The hole at Blaenavon, looking for the first ever viaduct, was the biggest one I've ever dug – it really would take some beating. I would have loved to have made it bigger and to have really got down to that bridge. It is just so tantalizing to think that it must be there. And in that entire hole there were just two phases: the industrial waste from the nineteenth-century mining and the 1970s domestic refuse on the top. Because of the scale of the excavation, it was a matter of winding up the mechanical-digger drivers and getting them digging. Nowadays it's so easy to dig a big hole because all that is needed is two big diggers that do what is called 'haymaking': one moves the spoil on to one level and the other moves it on to the surface.

A popular misconception is that all industrial sites have technical drawings, usually by landowners or builders, that show their plans, but often this isn't the case. I remember working on the Kennet and Avon Canal and digging an early lock. There were no plans and my best source of information, certainly for anything above the water, was a painting by Constable. I became a convert to him overnight. Even when there are plans, archaeologists excavate the sites in the normal way, looking at the layers, trying to unravel their sequence and making sure they are all recorded and their extent is known.

Antiquarians started to dig sites around the eighteenth and nineteenth centuries. I love following their excavations. One of the most memorable *Time Team* digs in this respect was at Lambeth Palace in London, even if we were dealing with a relatively recent excavation – in the 1930s the archaeologist Bernard Davis had claimed that he had found gravels from a Roman road (Watling Street) in the palace garden. It was great to be able to drop in on his trench and look at his section. I take my hat off to him: the published section was spot on. I had no problems with that at all. Where he had fallen down was on his interpretation. That's not a bad problem; it's not his fault, he just got it wrong. He was looking at natural gravel and thought it came from a Roman road – simple mistake. I just happened to have a wry smile on my face.

this simple sequence you get further categories with bronze axes developing from a simple flat axe to a palstave to a socketed axe. Whilst this method is good as a means of getting a rough date – an idea of what period you are looking at or whether one layer or site is older than another – it doesn't give you a firm date, which is where absolute dating processes became invaluable.

When investigating more recent sites, such as the eighteenth and nineteenth centuries, typological dating is much more useful as artefacts such as pottery, can be dated using historical documents or by looking at the potter's mark, thus pinning the sequence down to absolute dates. This period also saw a higher frequency of change in styles, allowing dates to be more precise.

Coin Blanks

Coins have been made and used in Britain for about 2,000 years and for most of this time they were produced by stamping designs on either a pre-cast metal blank or one that had been cut out from a sheet of metal. It was a laborious process, done by hand, and involved using punched dies – like the one *Time Team* found at York – to apply the obverse and reverse designs to the blank.

Coins were mass-produced for the first time in 1788 when Matthew Boulton, a manufacturer and engineer, introduced steam-powered coining presses in his factory at Soho in Birmingham: blanks cut from sheets of copper alloy were fed into the presses and stamped with standardized designs. These coin blanks were found during our excavation at Soho, and date from the late eighteenth and nineteenth centuries.

Kiln Furniture and Pot Wasters

To fire clay pots to a temperature high enough to make them hard, or to harden a glaze surface (essentially a thin layer of 'glass'), a kiln had to be heated, usually by a fire under the chamber containing the pottery, and kept at a certain temperature. The pots rested on some sort of perforated floor or support of ceramic bars so that hot air and gases could pass between them. Kiln furniture also included small clay stands and bars which were used to keep glazed items apart – if the pots touched each other the glaze would fuse them together.

Accidents often occurred during firing: pots might explode because the clay contained air pockets or was poorly tempered, or because temperatures varied in different parts of the kiln. Or glazed pottery might stick to the kiln furniture. Unless the potter was very careful, there was always a percentage of bent and broken pieces of pottery – and although fragments could be, and frequently were, used as spacers in early kilns, most of these pot wasters were of no use and were usually discarded.

Waste pottery and pieces of kiln furniture on a site indicate the existence of kilns and a pottery industry Here you can see the outline of the kiln *Time Team* found at Burslem, Stoke-on-Trent during our investigation into Josiah Wedgwood's first kiln.

Mick on... Early Modern sites

The major Time Team sites from the industrial period were Burslem in Stoke-on-Trent, Soho in Birmingham and Blaenavon in south Wales. The first two gave us a real feel for the impact the development of industry had on people and places, with the massive scale of pottery production in Burslem and Matthew Boulton's mint in Soho. We also had to deal with the difficulties involved in digging on an urban site, much like those we would face if we excavated in Timechester. Blaenavon was a totally different experience. Here *Time Team* was looking for the earliest viaduct in Britain. It had been buried under waste rock and slag, and the entire landscape around the site had been altered with valleys filled in and new hills created. The industrial period saw monumental landscape change and manipulation.

Industrialization developed either because a place had a tradition of production or manufacture and expanded by attracting investment and workers, or because a particular industry was spurred on by an individual. The most obvious entrepreneurs are George and Richard Cadbury in Birmingham, Joseph Rowntree in York, Josiah Wedgwood in Stoke-on-Trent and Sir Jesse Boot in Nottingham. Men like these employed huge numbers of people, which led to what was probably the most distinctive feature of the industrial period: areas of court, or back-to-back, housing – the sort of places that had one privy (lavatory)

to 100 families. They were built from about 1800 and were the result of the need to cram factory workers into small spaces. This is the period I would least like to have lived in. However, land was often allocated for parks with trees, lawns and bandstands. This was very typical of the nineteenth century and, by and large, it doesn't happen with modern developments: we just leave SLOAPs, Space Left Over After Planning – the areas with 'no ball games' signs.

If I were looking down at Timechester, I'd see an earlier street plan with enclosed fields (eighteenth- to nineteenth-century if the town was in the Cotswolds) and hedgerows in the surrounding countryside. However, the extent to which history has been damaged in the last fifty years can be surprising, and the best way to uncover it is to go back to the 1880s Ordnance Survey maps (1:500 and 1:10,000 scales). The imprint of history on towns was still so well preserved then that a map from 1,000 years earlier wouldn't provide much more information. Most of the damage to places and buildings is the result of the redevelopment schemes of the last twenty to thirty years.

Most road names would probably have survived and would indicate the destinations of some streets, the trades that were associated with others or who laid them out. The oldest building that is likely to be visible from a helicopter is the church. In Timechester it was originally built during Saxon times and rebuilt in the Middle Ages, like St Mary's Cathedral at Coventry, which was rebuilt in the fifteenth century. Many churches like the one at Timechester were restored in the nineteenth century, either well or badly depending on when this was done and who did it, and survive as perpendicular structures with tall towers or spires.

CHAPTER 10

present day

carenza's story of Timechester in 2000

The dawn of the new millennium in 2000 was only one of more than 450 such dawns that the Time Valley has seen since humans first set foot there, but nonetheless it was a landmark for Timechester, which is looking both back to its past and forward to its future. The two centuries since 1800 have seen many changes, and more are to come. Once again, the town has grown vastly in size; much of the countryside around Sutton Manor is now built-up, and there is little unoccupied land in the corridor between Timechester and Timemouth. A railway snakes its way up the valley and several new roads have appeared, sweeping through the landscape: Timechester is encircled by dual carriageways and roundabouts. One smaller road leads up to a car park near the hillfort, which is now owned by the town council and open to the public as a country park. Surprisingly, more seems to survive of the town walls and twin towers of the gates than before. The high street still follows its long-established line, but the gardens behind the houses that front on to the street are small. The town hall still stands on one side of the marketplace, but the area adjacent to the church is much changed, with a partly demolished large square building containing a tatty range of shops

The old street plan has completely vanished. Further away, the Moulton factory has mostly disappeared and its site is now occupied by terraced housing, but the kilns of Spodewood's potworks still stand overlooked by a multistorey car park, although they are no longer belching out black smoke. Archaeological excavations are taking place in several parts of the town. What has happened at

Timechester over the last two centuries to finally create the town of 2000?

The Victorian period was one of great industry that led to prosperity for some Timechester families, but to poverty and squalor for many more. The railway, which came to the town in 1855, was a boon for manufacturing but increased pressure on land and housing. The area behind the housing plots along the high street soon became a shanty town to accommodate workers in this yard, but in about 1900 much of it was cleared and a grid of new, neatly laid-out stone-built workers' housing was constructed.

Not all the housing in Timechester was so well-designed and built. Across the river, Moulton's factory was pulled down in about 1880 when the works moved to a larger site further out of the town, and the site was sold off for more cheap back-to-back housing. This created a large amount of living space, but at great cost: the houses were built on former marshland, which was damp and unsanitary, and were prone to shift and crack. They were dark with rarely a breath of fresh air. Despite this, ever-increasing numbers of people crowded into them, far more than the rudimentary sanitary facilities could accommodate. With up to a hundred people sharing one tap and one lavatory, disease was rife.

opposite: walmgate in modern day York, the old town of the viking period now only accessible through deep excavation

Timechester was severely bombed in the Second World War and during the subsequent reconstruction the worst of the back-to-back slum housing was pulled down and new estates were built, many on the margins of the town. The centre of Timechester, also badly damaged, was rebuilt in the 1950s and included a brand-new shopping centre whose layout completely ignored the plan of the medieval town. However, the line of the town walls was deemed ideal for the new ring road that was built to divert increasingly large numbers of cars away from the town centre.

But Timechester's historic heritage wasn't totally ignored: towards the end of the twentieth a considerable amount of public money was spent on restoring the town walls and gates and purchasing Timebury Hill. This was opened to the public as a country park where people could go for a walk and enjoy the ancient monument that had overlooked the town for so long. They could also get a fine view of the new motorway that was being constructed across the valley.

In the 1970s and 1980s the final decline of manufacturing industry, which had been an increasingly uncomfortable fact for decades, plunged Timechester into recession. Many shops in the shopping centre struggled to survive, and most were dealt a final blow when an out-of-town shopping mall opened beyond the ring road. Much of the centre of the town became almost derelict and the old town hall, for which the council could find little money and no use, became a target for vandals.

However, at the dawn of the second millennium AD, things may be looking up. Grants from the government and the European Union have been directed to Timechester to help it rebuild itself. In advance of the construction of new offices, houses and shops in many parts of the town and its hinterland, archaeological investigations are under way. What evidence will they find for nearly half a million years of Timechester's past?

Look out for the Time Team in a town near you

conclusion

I hope you have enjoyed this journey through Timechester's past. Some of Victor's pictures and Carenza's stories may have seemed familiar. One of the joys of living in Britain is the way the evidence from thousands of years of history has left its mark and can be seen by enthusiastic searchers, who may have to go no further than their own back gardens. In just one of the programmes in the 2000 series, at Alderton in Northamptonshire, at lunchtime of Day Two we were looking at medieval floor tiles, Roman pottery and a Saxon knife, all within 10 metres (33 feet) of the locals' homes. So this kind of rich historical evidence can turn up not only in the obvious locations, but also close to people's homes.

Mick and Tony on Salisbury plain, during filming in 2000

Time Team is about the history you can find on your doorstep, and somewhere close by you will find the traces of a medieval street, the remains of a road that was once the route of Roman legions and the lumps and bumps of a settlement once occupied by our prehistoric ancestors.

Archaeologists like Mick and Carenza who specialize in the landscape often refer to it as being something you can read. One of the most interesting elements that has emerged during our reconstruction of Timechester has been how it is possible to identify traces of the medieval past in particular, and even the Saxon period, in the street plans and maps of many English towns and villages. Going through Phil, Mick and Carenza's references to this subject in their sections on archaeological techniques has made me realize how easy it is to take for granted something as obvious as mapwork when you begin to enquire into the past of an area. It is perhaps not as glamorous or exciting as plucking bits and pieces from trenches, but it is essential in setting out the context for the whole site. This kind of work, done by Stewart Ainsworth and Bernard Thomason on Time Team, is often crucial

to our understanding of a site. If I were planning an excavation in Timechester now, I would definitely spend more time on maps and survey work than we are generally able to do for most of the programmes.

I would also spend more time looking at Timechester's prehistoric past. Because *Time Team* tends to work back from a good story connected to a good set of more recent artefacts, we often find it difficult to locate early prehistoric sites that fit the bill. I have always tried to include them because they represent such a

Mr phil Harding in action

crucial element in the story of our past– and are a real challenge to the skills of the Team. If they work well they are also capable of producing real revelations for viewers, who are often unaware that mammoths roamed the swamps now crossed by the M4, that cave dwellers made flint tools near Sheffield or that glaciers from the last Ice Age left massive gashes in the earth that can still be seen as many of the upland valleys today.

Whatever period we choose for a particular programme, I hope this story of one imaginary town's past has shown that excavation is a vital part of understanding the secrets of any particular time in our history. A sad state of affairs existed in archaeology recently which suggested that digging might not be needed, that radar and geophysics could tell us all we needed to know, and that because all excavation was destructive we should cease to find out about what really survives and leave it in the archaeological equivalent of mothballs. Luckily people think differently now, but this attitude created a whole generation of archaeologists who believed it might be safer to speculate rather than excavate, and who were better at handling a pen than a trowel. It certainly seemed to generate a fair number of television programmes where theories were given credence because no one wanted to dig a decent trench to prove them wrong.

Things have begun to swing back the other way and it is to be hoped that if books like this, and programmes like *Time Team*, can demonstrate just one thing, it would be that excavation is crucial to our understanding of the past. No form of geophysics has yet been invented, or will ever be invented, that will be a substitute for a combination of the human eye, human brain and the delicate manipulation of the good old trowel. I hope that reading some of Phil's first-hand impressions of the excavation process will have given you an idea of just what an amazing combination of skill, physical dexterity and experienced judgement is required to practise the trade.

If there is one thing that keeps us all on our toes at every site we visit, it is the way each trench gradually gets its secrets unpicked by Phil, Carenza and the other diggers. As we begin peeling back the turf on Day One we never know quite what to expect, and it is this mystery of the unfolding evidence that still makes every programme so exciting for all of us. Each one pushes all the members of the Team, including those who are responsible for writing up and recording each site in detail after the excavation is completed, to the edge of their skills.

Tony shows Time Team's finds at Lindisfarne in 2000.

It would be nice to think that somewhere in Timechester's library there is a shelf where you could go and read about the various excavations in the town. Perhaps this would make you enthusiastic enough to want to join a dig – without the support of local people archaeology will struggle to survive. In general, *Time Team* sites are still suggested by members of the public, so we would be dependent on Timechester residents getting in touch and inviting us in. If this book has made you interested in archaeology, join a local archaeological or historical group or the *Time Team* club. Perhaps you might one day send a letter to us – somewhere near you, a bit of 'Timechester' is waiting to be uncovered!

index

Page numbers in italics refer to photographs

Authors' and Editor's acknowledgments

We would like to thank a number of people whose help and support has been invaluable in producing this book. For their advice and assistance with the technical detail and archaeological content, thanks must go to: Guy de la Bédoyère, Andy Currant, John Gater, Peter Jones, Anna McOmish, David McOmish, Peter Reynolds and Bernard Thomason.

Special thanks to Ben Frow, *Time Team*'s Commissioning Editor at Channel 4 for his continuing support in the making of the *Time Team* programmes.

We are also grateful to Teresa Hall for sourcing and collating all the photographs, and for her assistance in correcting the final layout.

And finally, particular thanks to Kate Haddock for her tireless work in bringing it all together.

picture credits

The illustrations of Timechester by Victor Ambrus (of which details appear on other pages) are specially commissioned for this book: 12/13, 28/29, 42/43, 56/57, 72/73, 88/89, 104/105, 118/119, 132/133 and 144/145.

The cartoon of Phil Harding that appears on pages 21, 36, 48, 61, 79, 96, 110, 127 and 138, and the cartoon of Mick Aston that appears on pages 25, 39, 53, 68, 85, 101, 115, 129 and 141 are also specially drawn by Victor Ambrus.

The following photographs are by Mick Aston: 15, 16, 17, 18, 19, 20, 23, 24, 31, 32, 34, 35, 38, 44, 45, 47, 49, 50, 51, 52, 62, 63 (both), 64, 65, 66, 67, 74, 75, 77, 78, 80, 81, 82 (all), 83, 84 (both), 91, 92, 93, 94, 95, 97, 99, 100, 106, 108, 109, 111, 112, 113, 114, 120, 122, 124, 125, 126, 128 (both), 134, 135, 136, 139, 140 and 147.

The photograph on page 137 is by Chris Bennett.

The following photographs are by Paul Stokes and are provided courtesy of Channel 4: 6, 9, 58, 146, 148, 149, 150 and 151.

Behind the Scenes at Time Team

Tim Taylor
Photographs by Chris Bennett

0 7522 7226 8
paperback, 192 pages, £12.99

In this, the first *Time Team* book, Tim Taylor, the series producer, uses a series of case studies from the sixth series of *Time Team* – Cooper's Hole near the Cheddar Gorge, dating back to 10,000 BC, sixteenth-century docklands in Kent, Josiah Wedgwood's first kiln, Roman ironworks near Battle and the crash site of a Second World War bomber in Norfolk – to provide an insight into the initial choice of site and background research, through the trials and tribulations of filming the dig, to post-production work.

Tim seeks to create a full picture of life on location. For each site he describes the archaeological techniques used, the strategies employed by the Team and the problems they faced when things didn't turn out as expected.

With complete access behind the scenes, Chris Bennett has captured many shots that reveal the tensions and human drama of each three-day dig.

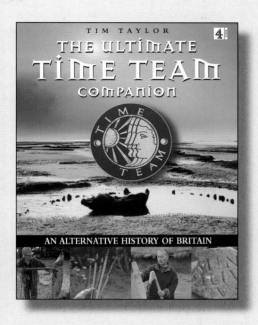

The Ultimate Time Team Companion
Tim Taylor

0 7522 1819 0
hardback, 216 pages, £20.00

This book provides the ultimate guide to all the excavations *Time Team* has featured, showing our history at its most fascinating from the dawn of time to the modern age.

In *The Ultimate Time Team Companion*, Tim Taylor draws on the expertise of the *Time Team* contributors to answer all your questions about the programme. The book provides both a complete guide to the excavations in the series and a view of the history surrounding them.

Tim has also included five fascinating photo stories from the seventh series of *Time Team* in which they visited Cirencester to discover their first Roman mosaic; had a poignant trip to northern France to a site where an early Spitfire pilot plunged to his death; learned how to fire a musket at Basing House, a Royalist household held under siege for two years during the Civil War; as well as exploring the wetlands at Flag Fen – Britain's most famous Bronze Age site – and the Palaeolithic history of Elveden in Suffolk.

A selected list of books available
from Channel 4 Books

The prices shown below are correct at time of going to press. However, Channel 4 Books reserve the right to show new retail prices on covers which may differ from those previously advertised.

The Ultimate Time Team Companion	Tim Taylor	£20.00
Behind the Scenes at Time Team	Tim Taylor	£12.99
Secrets of the Dead	Hugh Miller	£16.99
Mysteries of Lost Empires	Marshall Jon Fisher and David E. Fisher	£18.99
The Crimean War	Paul Kerr	£6.99
Green and Pleasant Land	Steve Humphries and Beverley Hopwood	£6.99
Britain's Slave Trade	S.I. Martin	£6.99

All these titles can be ordered from your local bookshop or simply by ringing our 24-hour hotline on 01624 844444, email bookshop@enterprise.net, fax 01624 837033 or fill in this form and post it to Bookpost PLC, PO Box 29, Douglas, Isle of Man IM99 1BQ. Please make all cheques payable to Channel 4 Books or complete your credit/debit card details.

Name . . . .

Address . . . .

. . . . Postcode . . . .

Card Number: ☐☐☐☐ ☐☐☐☐ ☐☐☐☐ ☐☐☐☐

Card Name (please tick one):

Visa ☐   American Express ☐   Mastercard ☐   Switch ☐

Expiry date . . . . . / . . . . .   Issue number (Switch) . . . .

Signature . . . .

POSTAGE AND PACKING FREE FOR ALL ADDRESSES IN THE UK

www.panmacmillan.com   www.channel4.com